# DRIVER'S SURVIVAL HANDBOOK

## Wade Hoyt & Roy Doty

**PAUL WAHL** CORPORATION PUBLISHER

DRIVER'S SURVIVAL HANDBOOK

Published by
Paul Wahl Corporation
Bogota, NJ 07603-0500
Auto, WV 24917-0201

95   94   93   92   91   90   89   88      5   4   3   2   1

Library of Congress Card Number 87-51600
ISBN 0-943997-01-1

Editorial and production services:
Columbine, Inc., Blue Hill, Maine

# Contents

# How to Use This Book

*Driver's Survival Handbook* is intended for people who are turned off or intimidated by the typical car repair book. Most such books are written by and for people who already know a lot about cars. The typical "non-technical" car care book is written for people who know little about cars by people who may know even less.

The authors of this book have been car enthusiasts for decades, but haven't forgotten the millions of people out there who are not having a love affair with their cars...people who view their automobiles merely as overgrown, and often balky, appliances.

We have tried to make this book as easy to use as possible. It starts with a series of TROUBLESHOOTING tables that can help you track down the causes of many common car problems.

Next comes a table of recommended periodic maintenance procedures that can help keep your car trouble free.

This is followed by the heart of the book—alphabetized entries full of tips and info that will not only come to your aid when car trouble strikes, but help you to avoid it in the first place. You will find advice on nuts and bolts subjects from AIR BAGS to ZIPPERS, along with a wide variety of such "people problems" as police, assaults, parking lot etiquette, and tips for travelling with dogs, cats, and/or children. Whether you are stuck in snow or overheating, the answer's in *Driver's Survival Handbook*.

The best way to use this book is to first read it from

cover to cover and follow its preventive maintenance advice. Then keep it in your glove compartment for ready reference in case of trouble. You'll wonder how you survived all these years without it!

# Read This First!

The material in this book is of a general nature applicable to most cars. It is not intended to replace the specific information in your Owner's Manual, which should always be followed to the letter.

Working on your car can be dangerous unless you follow these commonsense rules:

• Never work on a car if you are tired, intoxicated, ill, or taking drugs.

• Don't wear a necktie, rings, dangling jewelry, or loose clothing when working on a car. Tie back long hair or keep it under a hat so it can't get caught in moving parts. Jewelry can cause electrical shorts that may shock or burn you.

• Keep clear of fan blades in the engine compartment, even if they are not moving. Thermostatically controlled electric fans can start up without warning.

• Never run an engine indoors unless the work area is well ventilated and exhaust fumes can escape.

• If you will be working on the fuel system, or if you smell a gasoline odor, do not smoke, light a match, use a heater, turn on a light switch, or run a power tool, fan, or electric motor. All of these can cause sparks and an explosion. It is best never to work on the fuel system indoors.

• Disconnect the negative (-) battery cable whenever you work on the fuel or electrical system or near an electric radiator fan.

• Never cause sparks or a flame near the battery, which can emit explosive hydrogen gas.

• Never heat a garage with a heater that uses a

flame. Use only electric heaters, and keep them far enough away that you won't accidentally kick them over.

• If you must work under a car, make sure it's on level ground, its wheels are chocked, and the parking brake is set. A manual transmission should be in FIRST or REVERSE, an automatic in PARK. Never work under a raised car unless it is supported by jack stands or ramps (cars often roll or fall off jacks).

• Catch all draining fluids in large, tip-proof containers that are used for nothing else. Wipe up spills immediately. Put soaked rags outdoors until flammable fumes evaporate, then dispose of them in closed metal containers to prevent spontaneous combustion. Follow all local environmental and safety regulations when you dispose of drained fluids.

• Keep all flammable, poisonous, and corrosive materials away from children, pets, and potential fire sources.

• Work in a well-lit area. If you use a "drop light," make sure it is enclosed in a cage so the bulb can't shatter if it's dropped. Do not use a drop light near flammable liquids. Do not use a drop light or any electrical tools or heaters near puddles, wet floors, or other moisture.

• If you don't have the required skills, tools, time, or work area needed to perform any job in this book, don't do it yourself.

• Use only parts recommended by your car maker, or replacement parts from a reputable auto parts company listed specifically for your make and model car. Avoid bargain no-name parts and pirated parts packaged to look like the car maker's original equipment.

• Keep a first aid kit handy for minor scrapes and

burns, and a fire extinguisher rated for Class A-B-C fires.

• Never work alone. An adult should be nearby to call for help in an emergency.

Don't let any of the above turn you off. Millions of people do light maintenance and repair work on their cars each year without serious injury. You can too, if you develop careful work habits, follow the safety rules above, and don't do anything not specifically recommended in your Owner's Manual.

# Troubleshooting

Use these tables to find the most likely causes of problems with your car. If the cure is covered in this book, you will find a cross reference to the appropriate entry, such as "(see ANTIFREEZE)." These entries are listed alphabetically after the Troubleshooting tables. If the cure to a problem is beyond the scope of this book, you will have to take the car to a mechanic. Before you do, be sure to read the following entries: MECHANICS; REPAIRS; TOW TRUCKS; and WARRANTIES.

## Brake Problems

### Car pulls to one side when braking

1. Incorrect tire pressure; adjust tire pressure (see TIRE PRESSURE).
2. Brakes are wet from driving through deep puddles; dry brakes by putting light pressure on the pedal as you drive (see BRAKE FAILURE).
3. Wheels are out of alignment; have wheels aligned (see WHEEL ALIGNMENT).
4. Wheel bearings loose or worn; have a mechanic adjust or replace bearings.
5. Brakes need adjustment; see a mechanic.
6. Brake disc is warped; have a mechanic grind or replace the warped disc.
7. Worn or defective brake parts; have a mechanic inspect and repair brakes.
8. Grease or brake fluid on brakes; see a mechanic; have any fluid leaks repaired.

## Brakes do not stop car

1. Brake fluid level low; check fluid level and add more if it's low (see BRAKE FLUID). If problem is not cured, have car towed to a mechanic (see TOW TRUCKS).
2. Brakes overheated and faded; stop car and let brakes cool before driving (see BRAKE FAILURE).
3. Brakes wet from driving through deep puddles; dry brakes by putting light pressure on the pedal as you drive (see BRAKE FAILURE).
4. Air in hydraulic brake lines; have a mechanic bleed air from system and replace old fluid.
5. Brakes need adjustment; see a mechanic.
6. Worn or defective brake parts; have a mechanic inspect and repair brakes.

## Brake warning light stays on after starting engine

1. Brake fluid level low; check fluid level and add more if it's low (see BRAKE FLUID). If problem is not cured, have car towed to a mechanic (see TOW TRUCKS).
2. Air in hydraulic brake lines; have a mechanic bleed air from system and replace old fluid.
3. Worn or defective brake parts; have a mechanic inspect and repair brakes.
4. Electrical fault; have a mechanic check system.

## Brake warning light never comes on, even when starting engine

1. Electrical fault; have a mechanic check system.

### Brakes squeal

1. A high-pitched squeal during light braking is annoying but normal on some disc brake designs; ask the dealer to check the TSB file for a cure (see TECHNICAL SERVICE BULLETINS).
2. A loud squeal may be the low lining warning system found on some disc brakes; have a mechanic check the linings and replace them if necessary.
3. Worn or defective brake parts; have a mechanic inspect and repair brakes.

## Car Won't Start

### Engine does not crank

1. Automatic transmission is not in PARK or NEUTRAL; manual transmission clutch is not fully depressed; follow starting procedures in your Owner's Manual.
2. Battery is dead; jump start car (see JUMP STARTING) or recharge or replace battery (see BATTERY CHECKS, BATTERY RECHARGING, BATTERY SHOPPING).
3. Defect in electrical or starter system; see a mechanic.

### Starter cranks slowly; engine won't start

1. Battery is nearly dead; jump start car (see JUMP STARTING) or recharge or replace battery (see BATTERY CHECKS, BATTERY RECHARGING, BATTERY SHOPPING).
2. Defect in electrical or starter system; see a mechanic.

### Starter cranks normally; engine won't start

1. Out of gas; check fuel gauge (see OUT OF GAS).
2. Spark plug cables loose or defective; open hood, locate coil and spark plug cables, and push them on tight; if that doesn't help, see a mechanic.
3. Defect in electrical or starter system; see a mechanic.
4. Defect in carburetor, fuel injection, or fuel pump; see a mechanic.

## Car Stalls

### Engine stalls when cold

1. Fuel system icing; add fuel line antifreeze (see DRY GAS).
2. Choke needs adjustment; see a mechanic.
3. Carburetor or fuel injection system needs adjustment or repair; see a mechanic.
4. Spark plugs fouled; see a mechanic.
5. Clogged fuel filter or line; see a mechanic.
6. Dirt or water in gas; have tank drained and filters replaced.
7. Defect in carburetor, fuel injection or fuel pump; see a mechanic.
8. Engine needs a tuneup; see a mechanic.

### Engine stalls when hot

1. Carburetor flooded; wait five minutes, then hold gas pedal on floor without pumping to start car.
2. Vapor lock (hot weather only); open hood and let fuel pump and lines cool off for 10-15 min-

utes, then start car.

3. Air filter clogged; inspect and replace filter (see AIR FILTER).
4. Vacuum hose disconnected; check under hood for small disconnected hose and reconnect it, or see a mechanic.
5. Ignition timing incorrect; see a mechanic.
6. Choke needs adjustment; see a mechanic.
7. Carburetor or fuel injection system needs adjustment or repair; see a mechanic.
8. Spark plugs fouled; see a mechanic.
9. Clogged fuel filter or line; see a mechanic.
10. Dirt or water in gas; have tank drained and cleaned, filters replaced.
11. Defect in carburetor, fuel injection, or fuel pump; see a mechanic.
12. Engine needs a tuneup; see a mechanic.

## Car Rides Rough

1. Incorrect tire pressure; check and adjust (see TIRE PRESSURE).
2. Shock absorbers worn out; check shocks (see SHOCK ABSORBERS) and have them replaced if necessary.
3. Faulty suspension parts; have a mechanic inspect and repair suspension.
4. Springs sagging (older car); have helper springs installed or original springs replaced.
5. Car is overloaded; remove excess weight or have heavy-duty shocks and springs installed.

# Electrical Problems

## Lights don't work

*One light only*
1. Bulb burned out; replace bulb or headlight unit (see BULB REPLACEMENT, HEADLIGHTS).
2. Bulb socket corroded; remove bulb, clean socket with wire brush, try again.

*Several lights*
1. Fuse burned out; check fuse box (see FUSES).
2. Battery dead; check and recharge or replace battery (see BATTERY, BATTERY SHOPPING).
3. Alternator drive belt loose or broken; check and tighten or replace drive belt (see BELTS, BELT TIGHTENING).
4. Faulty switch, wiring, or ground; have a mechanic check electrical circuits.

## Turn signals don't work

*Signals flash too fast or only on one side of car*
1. Bulb burned out; replace bulb (see BULB REPLACEMENT).
2. Bulb socket corroded; remove bulbs, clean sockets with wire brush, try again.
3. Flasher unit burned out; replace flasher (see TURN SIGNALS).

*Signals don't flash at all*
1. Fuse burned out; check fuse box (see FUSES).
2. Flasher unit burned out; replace flasher (see TURN SIGNALS).
3. Battery dead; check and recharge or replace battery (see BATTERY CHECKS, BATTERY

RECHARGING, BATTERY SHOPPING).

4. Faulty switch, wiring, or ground; have a mechanic check electrical circuits.

## Any electrical part does not work

1. Fuse burned out; check fuse box (see FUSES).
2. Battery dead; check and recharge or replace battery (see BATTERY CHECKS, BATTERY RECHARGING, BATTERY SHOPPING).
3. Faulty switch, wiring, or ground; have a mechanic check electrical circuits.

## Horn will not stop blowing

1. Horn switch stuck; silence horn (see HORN) and have mechanic check system.
2. Horn relay stuck; silence horn (see HORN) and have mechanic check system.
3. Faulty switch, wiring, or ground; have a mechanic check electrical circuits.

## Battery voltage low, battery dead

1. Check and recharge or replace battery (see BATTERY CHECKS, BATTERY RECHARGING, BATTERY SHOPPING).
2. Faulty switch, wiring, or ground; have a mechanic check electrical circuits.
3. Alternator drive belt loose or broken; check and tighten or replace drive belt (see BELTS, BELT TIGHTENING).
4. Alternator overloaded; don't use extra accessories (driving lights, etc.), or else have a heavy-duty alternator installed.
5. Defective alternator or voltage regulator; have

mechanic check entire battery charging system.

# Engine Problems

### Engine runs poorly

1. Air filter clogged; check and replace air filter (see AIR FILTER).
2. Carburetor icing (cold weather only); add fuel line antifreeze (see DRY GAS).
3. Out of gas; check fuel gauge (see OUT OF GAS).
4. Spark plug cables loose or defective; open hood, locate coil and spark plug cables, push them on tight; if that doesn't help, see a mechanic.
5. Vapor lock (hot weather only); open hood and let fuel pump and lines cool off for 10-15 minutes, then start car.
6. Ignition system wet; use paper towels or aerosol moisture dispersant to dry distributor and spark plug cables.
7. Poor grade of gasoline; switch to higher octane gasoline or have engine timing checked.
8. Vacuum hose disconnected; check under hood for small disconnected hose and reconnect it, or see a mechanic.
9. Battery drained; (see "Battery voltage low, battery dead," above).
10. Ignition timing incorrect; see a mechanic.
11. Choke needs adjustment; see a mechanic.
12. Carburetor or fuel injection system needs adjustment or repair; see a mechanic.
13. Spark plugs fouled; see a mechanic.

14. Clogged fuel filter or line; see a mechanic.
15. Dirt or water in gas; have tank drained, filters replaced.
16. Engine needs a tuneup; see a mechanic.
17. Engine needs repair; see a mechanic.

## Engine overheats

1. Coolant level low; add a 50/50 mixture of water and antifreeze to the radiator and coolant recovery tank (see ANTIFREEZE).
2. Insufficient antifreeze in coolant; test antifreeze concentration with a hydrometer (see ANTIFREEZE). If concentration is too weak, drain some coolant and add straight antifreeze, then retest.
3. Fan belt slipping or broken; check belt, adjust or replace if necessary (see BELTS, BELT TIGHTENING).
4. Ignition timing incorrect; see a mechanic.
5. Burst or leaking radiator hose; check all coolant hoses and replace damaged ones (see HOSES).
6. Bad thermostat; have a mechanic check thermostat.
7. Bad radiator cap; check pressure cap on radiator or coolant recovery tank. Replace cap if gaskets are damaged, or if spring is broken or badly corroded. Have a mechanic pressure-test cap, or just replace it. Make sure replacement cap has the same pressure rating as the original.
8. Radiator leaking; check for leaks. Have a mechanic pressure-test radiator; repair or replace it.

9. Engine damage; have a mechanic check for faulty pollution control equipment and internal engine damage.

# Steering Problems

### Car pulls to one side

1. Incorrect tire pressure; check and adjust (see TIRE PRESSURE).
2. Wheels out of alignment; have wheel alignment checked (see WHEEL ALIGNMENT).
3. Brakes defective (see "Brake Problems," above).
4. Tires mismatched or worn unevenly; replace tires (see TIRE REPLACEMENT).
5. Suspension defective; see a mechanic.
6. Steering defective; see a mechanic.
7. Frame bent; have frame checked (see BODY SHOPS).
8. Wheel bearings loose; have a mechanic adjust.
9. Ball joints worn; have a mechanic replace ball joints.

### Steering wheel shimmies

1. Incorrect tire pressure; check and adjust (see TIRE PRESSURE).
2. Wheels are misaligned; have alignment checked (see WHEEL ALIGNMENT).
3. Wheels out of balance; have wheels balanced (see WHEEL BALANCE).
4. Tires have flat spots or other uneven wear patterns; check tire tread wear and check sidewalls for blisters; replace defective tires (see TIRE REPLACEMENT).

5. Shock absorbers worn out; test and replace shocks if necessary (see SHOCK ABSORBERS).
6. Suspension or wheel bearings loose, worn, or damaged; see a mechanic.

## Steering is difficult

1. Tires need air; check tire pressures (see TIRE PRESSURE).
2. Power steering fluid low; add power steering fluid (see POWER STEERING FLUID).
3. Power steering belt is slipping or damaged; (see BELTS, BELT TIGHTENING).
4. Steering linkage needs lubrication; have a mechanic grease steering linkage and check fluid level in steering gearbox.
5. Wheels are misaligned; have alignment checked (see WHEEL ALIGNMENT).
6. Suspension or wheel bearings loose, worn, or damaged; see a mechanic.

# Strange Noises

1. *Backfiring* may indicate improper ignition timing, faulty ignition system, or defective valves; see a mechanic.
2. *Clatter* from engine, especially when cold, may signal faulty valves or lifters, or a low oil level on engines with hydraulic valve lifters; check oil level first (see OIL LEVEL) or see a mechanic.
3. *Clicking* from wheels that changes with speed may mean a wheel cover is loose, there's a stone under the wheel cover, or the wheel bearing is bad. Check under wheel covers first

(see TIRE CHANGING), then see a mechanic if necessary.

*Clicking* from under the hood may be a bent fan blade hitting the radiator; check under hood with engine running, but don't touch fan! Have a mechanic repair a bent fan.

4. *Groan* from front wheels as car is steered may be due to low power steering fluid level; check fluid level and add more if necessary (see POWER STEERING FLUID).

5. *Hiss* from any part that is under pressure (tires, exhaust system) or a vacuum (hoses) indicates a leak; see a mechanic.

6. *Rattle* from under a rear-drive car, especially when accelerating or climbing hills, may indicate worn U-joints; see a mechanic.

*Rattle* from engine when accelerating or climbing hills is called "pinging"; switch to higher octane gas or have engine tuned (see PINGING).

7. *Roar* from under the car when engine accelerates means muffler or exhaust pipes have rusted out; have a mechanic inspect and repair system immediately, before anyone is poisoned by carbon monoxide gas.

8. *Scraping* when brakes are applied is a sign of worn brake linings; have a mechanic inspect brakes.

9. *Squeal* when wheels are turned means that the power steering pump's drive belt is slipping; tighten or replace belt (see BELT TIGHTENING).

*Squeal* from engine compartment when engine is accelerated indicates that other belts are loose; tighten or replace belts (see BELT TIGHTENING).

# Transmission Problems

### Automatic shifting is erratic or harsh

1. Transmission fluid low; check level and add fluid if necessary (see TRANSMISSION FLUID).
2. Transmission fluid burned or contaminated; have fluid and filter replaced by a mechanic.
3. Shift linkage needs adjustment.
4. Transmission bands need adjustment.
5. Vacuum hoses leaking or disconnected; have mechanic check hoses and modulator (if any).
6. Internal transmission damage; have transmission rebuilt or replaced.

### Manual transmission clutch slips

1. Clutch out of adjustment; have clutch adjusted.
2. Clutch worn, damaged, or contaminated with oil or grease; have clutch inspected and repaired.

### Manual transmission hard to shift

1. Clutch needs adjustment.
2. Clutch worn or damaged; have clutch inspected and repaired.
3. Shift linkage needs adjustment.
4. Transmission oil level low; have level checked and correct lubricant added.
5. Internal transmission damage; have a mechanic check and repair transmission.

# Preventive Maintenance

This list of regular checks and maintenance procedures can help to avoid trouble with most cars. This list is for the hypothetical *average* car, if such a thing exists. It is meant to give you an idea of what's involved in proper car care. You should follow the specific maintenance recommendations and intervals that are spelled out in your Owner's Manual.

Here's what to do and when to do it:

### Every time you get gas

1. Check engine oil level (see OIL LEVEL).
2. Check coolant level in radiator recovery tank (see ANTIFREEZE).
3. Check level of windshield washer fluid; add more if necessary.

### Every month

1. Check tire pressures (see TIRE PRESSURE).
2. Examine tires for tread wear or damage (see TIRE REPLACEMENT).
3. Check pavement under car for leaks (see LEAKS, FLUID).
4. Make sure all lights work; fix any that don't (see BULB REPLACEMENT, HEADLIGHTS).

### Every 3 months or 3000 miles (whichever comes first)

1. Change engine oil and filter (see OIL TYPES).
2. Have chassis lubricated (if it has lube points).
3. Have fluid level checked in manual transmission, differential, and hydraulic clutch (if any).

## Every spring and fall

1. Check all fluid levels; add proper fluid if necessary (see ANTIFREEZE, BRAKE FLUID, POWER STEERING FLUID, TRANSMISSION FLUID).
2. Check all drive belts; adjust loose ones, replace damaged ones (see BELTS).
3. Check all radiator and coolant hoses; replace any that are damaged or leaking (see HOSES).
4. Check battery (see BATTERY CHECKS).
5. Rotate tires (see TIRE ROTATION).
6. Check exhaust system for rust-outs and leaks; have defective parts replaced immediately.
7. Check rubber boots on front-drive axles for cracks or tears; have damaged boots replaced and the CV joints they protect inspected.

## Once a year

1. Have brakes inspected for damage and wear (twice a year if you do mostly stop-and-go driving).
2. Lubricate all hinges and locks.
3. Test shock absorbers (see SHOCK ABSORBERS).
4. Have headlight aim checked and adjusted.
5. Check air filter (see AIR FILTER).
6. Have wheel alignment checked (see WHEEL ALIGNMENT).
7. Spray weatherstripping around doors and trunk with silicone preservative.

## Every four years

1. As a precaution, replace all drive belts and hoses that haven't been replaced previously (see BELTS, BELT TIGHTENING, HOSES).
2. Have brake system bled and replace brake fluid.
3. Have automatic transmission fluid and filter replaced.

# Acceleration
## Sudden and unintended

A frightening type of accident involving cars with automatic transmissions has been baffling victims and experts alike. The accidents are all pretty much the same: the driver starts the car, shifts from PARK or NEUTRAL into either DRIVE or REVERSE, and the car simply takes off. The driver leaps onto the brake pedal, but the car just keeps going until it hits something. Numerous accidents and several deaths have been reported, involving many different makes of car.

Any car with automatic transmission will begin to move if you shift it into gear without holding one foot on the brake pedal. On a cold morning, an engine may idle at 2500 to 3000 rpm when it's first started—about half its top speed. If you shift into gear then, the car will suddenly lurch forward or backward, unless you plant your foot firmly on the brake pedal *before* you shift. (Here's a good reason to put your safety belt on before you start the engine.)

Car makers have claimed that panicky drivers have been unintentionally stomping on the gas pedal instead of the brake when their cars have suddenly lurched forward or backward.

If your car takes off suddenly:

1) Turn the ignition switch off, but not all the way to the LOCK position, which can lock the steering wheel.

2) Jump onto the brake pedal with *both* feet. If your pedal is too narrow, use your *left* foot only—you're less likely to hit the gas pedal by mistake with your left foot.

3) Report any sudden acceleration incident to the car maker and to the National Highway Traffic Safety

Administration's toll-free hotline: (800) 424-9393.

# Accidents
## How to handle

Even if no one is injured, an accident can be very up-setting. It is important to remain calm and think clearly. You may have to deal with another driver who is hurt, upset, or hostile. If you do the wrong thing, you may worsen an injury or help cause another accident in passing traffic.

Always keep the legal aspects of an accident in mind. Never admit guilt or apologize for the accident. Don't leave the scene until you have all the information your lawyer and insurance company will need. If there are injuries or serious damage, don't leave the scene until the police arrive—doing so may leave you open to criminal charges. Here's what to do:

1) Get your car well off the road, if possible. If the accident is on a city street, park at the curb to get out of

the flow of traffic. Turn off the ignition in every car involved to reduce the chance of fire. Place flares or reflective triangles (if you have them) along a highway to warn off traffic.

2) If you have certified first aid training, treat the injured until professional help arrives. If not, leave the injured alone and send for help. *Never* move an injured person unless he or she is in further danger from fire, leaking gasoline, or traffic.

3) Send for the police if there are any injuries, if there is serious damage, or if the other driver is hostile. Send for an ambulance if there are injuries, and for the fire department if there is leaking fuel or a fire.

4) Take down the names, addresses, and phone numbers of everyone involved, including passengers in each car and any witnesses.

5) Exchange licenses and registrations with all the other drivers and write down the following information for each one: name, address, driver's license number and expiration date, plus each car's license plate number, make, model, year, color, and body style (sedan, wagon, convertible, etc.). Note which driver was in which car.

6) Get the name and phone number of each driver's insurance company. If your state requires insurance I.D. cards, copy the information on each card.

7) Record the name and badge number of any police officers on the scene. If the police ask what happened, do not admit guilt. If you are unsure of how the accident happened, don't admit that, either.

8) Make a sketch of the scene, showing each car involved, its direction of travel, and all street names.

# Accident Reports
## When and how to file

In most areas, you have to file an accident report with the authorities if you've had an accident that involves more than one car, if there are any injuries, or if damages exceed a given amount. Ask the police or your insurance agent if you need to file a report, and how much time you have to do it.

You also may have to file a report with your insurance company, even if you don't intend to file a claim or sue the other driver(s). Both these reports may be used in court, so they should agree in every detail.

If you are not sure whether to file a report, ask your insurance agent. The report gives your version of the accident. It's usually a good idea to get that on the record in case the other driver decides to file a report or to sue.

Never take another driver's word that he won't file a report. And bear in mind that filing a report does not automatically mean your insurance rates will go up, especially if you don't file an insurance claim (see INSURANCE CLAIMS).

Most reports have a blank map that you can fill in with the names of streets and intersections at the accident scene. Show every car involved in the accident as a little box (label them A, B, C, etc.). Use arrows to show their direction of travel just before the accident, and show where each one wound up after the accident. Refer to the notes you made at the scene (see ACCIDENTS).

# Air Bags
## Pop! You're saved!

By Federal law, all 1990 cars must be equipped with "passive restraints" in the form of air bags or automatic seat belts (see SEAT BELTS, PASSIVE). Air bags are large inflatable pillows concealed in the steering wheel hub. They are designed to inflate in accidents at speeds above 12 mph, to protect the driver from the "second collision" of his body with the interior of the car. Sensors behind the bumpers ignite an explosive device that generates gas to inflate the pillow almost instantaneously. To be most effective, the driver must wear seatbelts to keep from glancing off the pillow.

Air bags are not a cure-all. They offer little or no protection in side impacts, rollovers, or rear-end collisions. Optional air bags can cost $800 or more, and re-arming them after a collision can run upwards of $1000.

Air bags do offer an extra margin of protection when the standard lap-shoulder safety belts are also worn. Safety belts can stretch under the tremendous force of an accident, and the driver often hits the steering wheel, resulting in chest, facial, and back injuries. Air bags prevent or reduce such injuries, but only if you buckle up.

# Air Conditioner
How to keep your cool

A car air conditioner should be repaired only by a shop or car dealer equipped to work on this specialized accessory. The average gas station is not equipped to do more than check the belts and hoses or add refrigerant (Freon).

You can check the refrigerant level on some cars by looking at the system's sight glass—a metal cylinder or block with a small, round window in it. The sight glass (if your car has one) is mounted somewhere in the hoses and pipes that run from the compressor through the engine compartment. The compressor is one of the belt-driven accessories mounted near the engine. Like the power steering pump, the compressor has two hoses or pipes attached to it; but unlike the pump, the compressor does not have a fluid reservoir with a big screw-off filler cap.

Once you have located the compressor, trace one of its hoses forward to the condenser (near the radiator) and then back, looking for the little window. It is often found on top of a Thermos-sized cylinder called the receiver/dryer.

Clean off the sight glass, turn on the engine, and set the air conditioner controls for maximum cooling. After about five minutes check the sight glass. If the glass is clear, the system is either fully charged or empty. If cool air is coming out of the dash vents, the system is OK.

A few bubbles in the sight glass mean that the system may be low on refrigerant. If bubbles come and go as the air conditioner clutch cuts in and out, the system is OK. If there are lots of bubbles all the time, or the glass is cloudy, have an expert check the system. You can buy refrigerant and replacement kits in auto parts, discount and department stores, but the procedure is a complex and potentially dangerous one better left to a mechanic.

You can keep the seals in your air conditioning system from drying out and leaking by operating it for five minutes each week throughout the year. This should prevent trouble, or at least alert you to it long before summer so you can get it fixed before the air conditioner repair shops become overbooked.

## Air Filter

How to check it, when to chuck it

The air your engine breathes has to be filtered to screen out dust, grit, insects, and other harmful stuff. In the good ol' days, this was accomplished by a simple pleated paper filter screwed to the top of the carburetor. After several thousand miles of driving, this air filter can become clogged with dirt, which may lead to hard starting, stalling, or poor gas mileage.

On today's pollution-controlled cars, the air filter has evolved into a *system* called the air cleaner. The filter itself is mounted inside a metal or plastic housing festooned with vacuum hoses and ducts.

To change the filter, locate the air cleaner housing, remove its cover, lift out the filter, dust out the housing and drop in the new filter.

On most cars, the filter is inside a circular housing at the top of the engine. On some cars, the housing may be oval or rectangular, and it may be located alongside the engine. Aside from the engine itself, the air cleaner is one of the bigger things under the hood.

Open the clips or unscrew the wing nuts that hold down the air cleaner cover; then remove the cover and lift out the filter. If it is wet, damaged, or caked with dirt, replace it with a filter designed specifically for your car make, model, and engine. In an emergency, you can dislodge some of the dirt from an air filter by tapping it gently on the pavement.

On most cars the filter should be replaced every 15,000 miles.

# Antenna
## Keep those hits coming

Radio antennas are often broken off in car washes or by vandals. Always lower a telescoping antenna before you enter a car wash and when you park. One-piece mast antennas do not telescope, but they can be easily unscrewed and removed by hand or with a small wrench. A loose antenna can cause poor radio reception. Tightening the nut at the base of the antenna will secure it.

Replacement antennas are sold in auto parts stores. To remove a broken telescoping antenna, unscrew the nut at the base of the antenna. Hold onto the broken antenna so it doesn't fall down inside the fender. Remove the nut and all the parts under it. Use a thin screwdriver to reach through the hole in the fender and push down on one side of the swivel clamp so you can pull the antenna base and cable out of the fender.

If you're lucky, the cable will unplug from the antenna base. Plug in the new antenna, tilt the swivel clamp, and insert it through the hole in the fender. Then slip the other parts (gasket, insulator ball, cap, and nut) over the antenna and tighten the nut.

If the cable is permanently attached to the base of the old antenna, you will have to unplug the cable from the back of the radio, pull it out of the fender, and thread the new cable back to the radio. This is a major project in many cars; you may want to have a car stereo store do the work. If you do it yourself, tie a long string to the cable when you unplug it from the radio. After you pull the cable out of the fender, you can use this string to lead the new cable back to the radio.

## Antifreeze
### Checking your protection

Modern cars need antifreeze winter and summer. Antifreeze not only lowers the freezing temperature of water, but raises its boiling point, too. Antifreeze also contains rust inhibitors and a lubricant for the water pump. The coolant mixture in your radiator should be 50% to 70% antifreeze plus water. More than 70% antifreeze will reduce your protection and lead to overheating.

Check the coolant level in the radiator every time you open the hood to check the oil. Most cars have a plastic coolant recovery tank alongside the radiator that's marked HOT and COLD. The coolant inside the tank should be at or above the appropriate mark when the engine is hot (after driving) or cold (before it's first started).

If your car has no recovery tank, remove the radiator cap to check the coolant level. Do this only when the engine is cold—after it has been sitting several hours or overnight. Push down on the cap and turn it counter-clockwise to open it. There should be enough coolant inside the radiator to cover the core tubes. Replace the cap if its rubber gaskets are brittle or cracked.

If the coolant level is low, add a 50/50 mixture of antifreeze and water to the radiator or recovery tank. Use only antifreeze labelled as safe for use with aluminum parts (most modern engines have some aluminum). Check the coolant level for several days afterward; if it continues to drop, there is a leak in the system.

You can check the concentration of antifreeze in your coolant with a syringe-like tester called a hydrometer, sold in auto parts stores. More expensive hydrometers have a float with a scale. Less expensive models contain several small colored balls. To use either one, open the radiator cap (be sure the engine is cold!) and squeeze the rubber bulb on the hydrometer to draw coolant into the tester.

The number of balls that float in the less expensive hydrometer indicate the freezing point of the coolant (see the hydrometer's instructions). You can read the freezing point on the floating scale in higher-priced testers.

If the freezing point is too high, drain some of the

coolant from the radiator and add straight antifreeze (see below). Run the engine to mix the coolant, then let it cool before rechecking the concentration. If the coolant hasn't been replaced for a year or more, replace it.

## How to drain and replace

Once a year, you should drain the coolant and replace it with fresh antifreeze and water, or have this messy job done by a pro. To make sure you wind up with at least a 50% concentration of antifreeze, look up the capacity of the cooling system in your Owner's Manual. It should list the capacity in quarts. You will have to buy at least half that amount of antifreeze, which is sold by the gallon. If you have an odd amount of antifreeze left over, save it in case you need to add more during the year.

Place a large pan under the radiator to catch the coolant. Antifreeze is sweet-tasting and poisonous; do not leave it in puddles where children or animals can drink it.

Make sure the engine is cold! First, turn the heater's temperature control to HOT so the heater core will drain, too. Next, open the radiator cap. Use pliers to open the petcock or a wrench to open the plug at the bottom of the radiator, and let the old coolant drain out. Open any drain plugs on the engine block, as well.

When the coolant has drained, close all the plugs and the petcock, and fill the radiator with water. Put back the radiator cap and run the engine until the thermostat opens to circulate coolant out of the engine block. Drain the radiator and repeat the steps above until water flowing from the petcock is clear.

You can speed up this tedious process with a flushing tee that you splice into the heater hose. Follow the instructions that come with the tee to force the old coolant out of the system.

Drain the radiator, close the petcock, and add enough antifreeze to the radiator for a 50/50 concentration. If the radiator is still not full, add water. Add antifreeze to the COLD mark on the coolant recovery tank. Refit the radiator cap and run the engine to mix the coolant.

If you can't add enough antifreeze to the radiator for a 50/50 mix, open the flushing tee or remove the heater hose at the engine's water pump. As you add antifreeze to the radiator, clear water will be forced out of the tee or hose. When you have added enough antifreeze, close the tee or attach the hose and tighten its clamp.

Run the engine until the thermostat opens, then recheck the coolant level; it may drop as air bubbles trapped in the system accumulate in the radiator. Wait for the system to cool down, then add more coolant if necessary.

# Arbitration
## Preparing the groundwork

Formal arbitration is a recent phenomenon in disputes between consumers and car dealers, importers, or manufacturers. Arbitration is a voluntary program that can avoid the time and cost of a lawsuit. There are several arbitration programs available in different states, some of which are run by the state Attorney General's office (write to the Attorney General of the state where the problem occurred, in care of the state capital, to get details).

Chrysler and Ford run their own arbitration programs. You can get information about them by writing to: Chrysler Customer Satisfaction Board, Box 1919, Detroit, MI 48288 or Customer Assistance Office, Ford Parts and Service Div., P.O. Box 1902, Dearborn, MI 48121.

The National Auto Dealers Association administers an arbitration program called AUTOCAP for the following makes: Alfa Romeo, BMW, Fiat, Honda, Isuzu, Jaguar, Mazda, Mitsubishi, Nissan, Peugeot, Rolls Royce, Saab, Subaru, Toyota and Volvo.

The Better Business Bureau runs arbitration programs for American Motors, Audi, General Motors, Honda, Nissan, Peugeot, Porsche, Renault, Saab, Volkswagen and Volvo. The BBB will try to mediate a dispute before submitting it to arbitration. For details, contact your local Better Business Bureau (see phone book for the address).

Mercedes-Benz doesn't subscribe to an arbitration program, but is subject to any state programs that exist.

Some cars may be covered by two or more programs. Get all of the details on each program before you decide which to pursue. Some programs are binding on the dealer or car maker, but not on the consumer—this is the type you want. Others are binding on both parties, which means you have no recourse if the decision goes against you.

Before you decide on arbitration, you should exhaust all other avenues (see COMPLAINTS and LEMON LAWS). The dealer should have several chances to correct the problem. You should then write to the car company's Zone Manager. If they can't resolve the problem, try the Regional or District Office, and finally the car maker or importer.

Before going into arbitration, do your homework! Assemble copies of all the dealer's work orders, your complaint letters, and any replies. Prepare a log, showing when each step occurred and its outcome. Make copies of your log and all other paperwork for the panel members.

If the arbitration panel's decision is not satisfactory, you must reject it in order to sue the car maker. If the decision is binding, you generally cannot sue; i.e., once you have accepted the panel's settlement, you can only sue if the dealer does not comply with the decision. If the car breaks down again, you may go back to arbitration, or sue for a refund or replacement of your car.

# Assaults

How to handle street people

There are two kinds of people who sometimes approach drivers in urban areas—relatively harmless panhandlers and vicious muggers. The problem is, it's nearly impossible for a driver to tell one from the other until it's too late.

Panhandlers may offer to wash your windshield for a tip. Some are professionally equipped with squeegees and buckets of soapy water; others wield greasy rags from the nearest garbage can. Even those who do a good job may get surly if they think your tip is too small. The best advice is not to deal with strangers, and never open your window to talk to them or give them money. Make sure all doors and windows are closed and locked before you leave home. Never unlock power door locks to get out of the car and confront a panhandler; all the doors would be unlocked at once, and an accomplice could enter the car from the passenger side.

Wave windshield cleaners off vigorously, shake your head "no," and form the word with your lips. Don't simply try to avoid eye contact—you'll find your windshield halfway "washed" before you know it and a belligerent panhandler demanding payment. If the lout doesn't get the message, turn on your windshield wipers and washer, while shaking your head.

If you see windshield washers at a red light far enough ahead, you may avoid them altogether by hanging back until the light turns green, and then driving by them without having to stop. The same strategy sometimes works with potentially dangerous hitchhikers and hookers.

Muggers specialize in smash-and-grab attacks on cars stuck in traffic. They will smash a window with a rock, grab a briefcase, camera bag, or purse, and run off before you can do anything. They often prey on women driving alone in expensive cars. Always keep purses, briefcases, camera bags, shopping bags, and other valuables out of sight—under a seat, or in the glove compartment or trunk. If someone attacks your car, drive off immediately, even if you have to run a red light or jump the curb—but only if you can do so without injuring bystanders or causing an accident.

# B

## Battery Checks
### Looking for signs of life

The usual cures for a dead battery are to jump-start the car from one with a good battery (see JUMP STARTING), or to recharge the battery (see below). Sometimes an apparently dead battery is fine, except for corrosion on the battery terminals, which reduces or blocks the flow of current.

If you see greenish-white deposits around the terminals at the ends of the battery cables, remove the cables from the battery terminals. Clean the terminals and cable connections with a wire brush or sandpaper until the metal is shiny, then reinstall the cables.

If a battery has removable caps, open them and check the fluid level inside. Fluid should cover the metal plates inside the battery, and come up nearly to the bottom of the filler holes. If the fluid is low, add distilled water slowly to bring it up to the correct level. (Distilled water is often sold in supermarkets or drug stores for use in steam irons.) In freezing weather, drive the car after adding water so that it mixes with the acid; if you don't the water could freeze and damage the battery.

You can check the charge of the battery with a relatively inexpensive device called a battery hydrometer. Follow the instructions that come with the syringe-like tool to draw some acid from each of the battery's six cells and determine its state of charge.

Sealed, maintenance-free batteries often have an "eye" or window with a built-in hydrometer. If the battery is OK, the eye is green. When the battery needs a charge, the eye looks dark. If the eye looks clear or pale yellow, the battery is low on fluid and cannot be safely recharged.

A battery loses much of its power in cold weather, but recovers it when the battery warms up. Sometimes an old, weak battery that can't start an engine on a cold morning will work after it has sat in the sun for several hours. You can heat the battery overnight to keep up its strength (electric battery heaters that run on house current are sold in cold climates for this purpose). You can also heat the battery by placing a 100-watt bulb in a drop lamp under the battery overnight. If the engine still won't crank, you need a jump start or a charge (see JUMP STARTING, BATTERY RECHARGING).

# Battery Recharging
## When and how to do it

If your starter cranks slowly or if your instruments or headlights seem dim, the battery may need to be recharged, preferably using a trickle charger overnight. You can also charge the battery by driving the car at highway speeds for several miles, as long as the alternator and charging system are working properly. A service station or repair shop can quick-charge a dead battery in less than an hour, but repeated quick-charges can damage the battery. If your battery needs frequent charging, it may be reaching the end of its life, or the charging system may be faulty. Have a mechanic check it.

First, check the battery's state of charge and fluid level (see BATTERY CHECKS). If the "eye" of a maintenance-free battery is clear or pale yellow, don't try to recharge the battery. If it needs recharging, use a trickle charger. Always wear eye protection when working on a battery. Disconnect the battery's negative cable. Then connect the charger's black clamp to the negative battery post and the red clamp to the positive post. Remove vent caps from a refillable battery. Now plug the charger in and turn it on.

Do not attach or remove the charger's clamps while the charger is running. This will cause a spark that may ignite explosive hydrogen gas given off when the battery is charged. Never smoke or light a match near a battery.

Let the charger run for several hours, until its meter reads less than one amp. Turn the charger off and unplug it before you remove the clamps. Then reconnect the negative battery cable and refit the vent caps (if any).

If the car still won't start, jump start it (see JUMP STARTING). If the engine can be jump started and the charging system warning light or ammeter on the dash indicates normal operation, the battery is too far gone to recharge and you should replace it.

The electrolyte inside a dead battery will sometimes freeze in very cold weather. Do not try to recharge a frozen battery. Instead, move the car or its battery to a warm area where the electrolyte can thaw, then recharge the battery.

## Battery Shopping
A heart transplant for your car

Replacement auto batteries are usually guaranteed to last three to six years, depending on their price, design, and quality. If you keep a car for more than three or four years, you'll probably be faced with having to buy a new battery. Since the guarantee varies with price, you should consider how much longer you intend to keep the car. If you plan to sell the car in a year or two, don't invest in an expensive five- or six-year battery.

There are two major types of battery—conventional and maintenance-free, plus a subspecies called low-maintenance, which is actually a conventional battery pretending to be something grander.

Car batteries develop 12 volts from a chemical re-action that takes place within six cells inside the bat-tery case. Each cell contains alternating positive and negative lead plates submerged in a mixture of water and sulfuric acid, called electrolyte. While this chemi-cal reaction goes on, water evaporates.

Conventional batteries have vent caps that allow this water vapor to escape. When the level of the elec-trolyte drops below the tops of the lead plates, battery voltage is reduced. Check the electrolyte level periodi-cally, adding distilled water when necessary.

Maintenance-free batteries let very little water va-por escape, so you never have to check the electrolyte level, and couldn't add water if you wanted to. Low maintenance batteries often have disguised vent caps that don't let much vapor escape. You can add water if you can figure out how to open the caps without break-ing them.

Batteries have several rating systems. The most useful is cold cranking power, which is listed in am-peres. A small engine may need only 250 amps to start it, a big V8 needs 400 amps or more. Check the cold cranking power of the battery that came with the car. If winter starting has been a problem, get a replacement with at least 20% more power. Some batteries have cable terminals on the top, others on the side. Get the same type of battery that came with your car so that the cables will fit.

## Belts
### Checking them out

The single fan belt on old-fashioned engines has been replaced by three to six drive belts on today's cars. These belts operate not only the water pump and fan, but also such accessories as the alternator (which charges the battery), the power steering pump, air conditioner compressor, and perhaps an air pump used in some pollution control systems. The belts turn pulleys to transfer power from the engine to the accessories.

Most drive belts have a V-shaped cross-section and are called V-belts. Other belts have a number of grooves that fit into a matching surface on special pulleys. Some cars use a single multi-groove belt that zigzags between all the accessories. A spring-loaded idler pulley keeps this serpentine belt tight.

Loose belts can squeal annoyingly, and slipping belts don't transmit full power to the accessories they drive. A slipping power steering belt may make steering difficult; a slipping alternator belt can drain the battery; a slipping water pump belt may lead to overheating; and so on. A cracked or worn-out belt may snap, stranding you on the highway when the accessory it drives stops working.

It's a good idea to carry spare drive belts in your car. If a belt breaks on the road and the nearest repair shop doesn't have a replacement in stock, they can quickly repair the car using your spare.

With the engine turned off and cool, check both sides of all belts regularly to make sure they are not cracked, brittle, glazed, or soaked with oil. If they are, have them replaced. You should replace all the belts every four years as a precaution—it might save you from a breakdown.

Also check the belt tension by pressing down on each belt with your thumb in the middle of the longest span between pulleys. If you can move the belt more than a half to three quarters of an inch, it needs to be tightened. If you can't budge it by even a quarter of an inch, it is too tight and may be putting too much stress on the accessory bearing.

## Belt Tightening
How to adjust or replace drive belts

To tighten a drive belt, loosen the mounting bolts on one of the accessories the belt drives. Place a pry bar, such as a crowbar or heavy pipe, between the accessory and the engine block. Then pull the accessory away from the engine while you tighten the mounting bolts. Be careful that you only pry against thick castings, and not against delicate fins or thin metal parts on the accessory. Re-check the belt tension and readjust if necessary.

Some accessories have an adjusting stud in addition to mounting nuts. They are mounted on large, flanged brackets. After loosening the mounting nuts, turn the nut on the adjusting stud clockwise to tighten the belt, and counter-clockwise to loosen the belt.

To replace a belt, loosen the mounting bolts on all accessories that the belt drives, and push them toward the engine. Pry the old belt off its pulleys. If there are other belts in the way, they must all be removed. (Check this out first—the job may be too complicated to do yourself.) Now you can roll the replacement belt onto the pulleys, first making sure the replacement is the correct one for your make, model, and year of car, and for the accessory involved. Once the belt is on the pulleys, tighten it as described above.

If a broken drive belt strands you on the road, you may be able to jury rig a replacement with a pair of pantyhose or nylon tights. Tuck the waistband and seat down into one of the legs, and twist the tights so that no loose ends can flap around and get caught in the other pulleys. Then stretch the pantyhose tightly around the pulley grooves of the missing belt and tie the ankles together firmly. If you drive slowly and don't rev the engine suddenly, this setup just might get you to the nearest service station.

To replace a serpentine belt, place a pry bar through the hole in the metal tab attached to the spring-loaded idler pulley. Push down on the pry bar to lift the idler pulley off the belt while a helper removes the belt. Place the new belt around all pulleys in exactly the same way as the original, making sure that the grooves in the belt match the grooves in the pulleys. There should be a decal in the engine compartment that shows the proper routing for a serpentine belt. Use the pry bar to lift the idler pulley while a helper places the belt under it. Then slowly lower the idler pulley onto the belt and remove the pry bar.

## Body Shops
Finding the right one for today's origami cars

"Bump shops" are a lot more sophisticated than they were in the days when almost every car had a separate body and frame. The vast majority of today's cars have unit-body construction, in which thin pieces of sheet metal are bent into box sections and welded together to form a single unit that supports the body, drivetrain, and suspension.

In a serious accident, parts of a unit-body car can fold up like an accordion. Although this absorbs some of the force of an accident and can help protect the passengers, the resulting damage is expensive and tricky to fix. A modern body shop needs a large piece of equipment, called a straightening bench, to accurately pull crunched unit-bodies back into shape. The straightening bench looks like a medieval torture rack with chains, hooks, and hydraulic cylinders that stretch out crushed bodywork. An experienced technician uses sophisticated measuring devices to make sure the unit-body is returned to its original dimensions.

Spot welds in the unit-body often pop during this stretching, and they must be re-welded using a Metal Inert Gas (MIG) welder; an old-fashioned arc welder or torch will not do the job.

Lastly, on front-drive cars, all four wheels should be re-aligned on a special four-wheel alignment machine. The rear wheels of a front-drive car can't be accurately aligned on a two-wheel machine.

Don't even consider a shop that isn't equipped with a straightening bench, MIG welder, and four-wheel alignment machine. Ask friends, relatives, and co-workers to recommend shops they have been happy with, and double-check those recommendations with the local Better Business Bureau.

A recent trend in accident repair is the use of new body parts made in Korea or Taiwan, rather than by the original car maker. These "aftermarket" parts are nearly as cheap as junkyard parts, but they are often made of inferior materials and therefore may rust through faster than original equipment parts. They also may not fit properly.

Insurance companies often insist on the use of aftermarket parts for accident repairs because they are cheaper. Car makers and most body shops oppose them, saying that the car owner gets a shoddy job when substandard parts are used. If the insurance company insists on aftermarket parts and you want factory pieces, you may have to pay the difference in price to the body shop. But you should at least get what you pay for: insist on seeing the parts and the body shop's invoice, to see if they are original factory parts or substitutes.

The whole process of getting an accident repair paid for by your insurance company is one that's ripe for corruption. An insurance adjuster who's on the take may recommend (or even insist) that you use a particular shop for your repairs. A body shop may offer to inflate its estimate or your bill so you can recover your deductible without the insurance company catching on.

Let your conscience be your guide in such negotiations, but remember: between the body shop, insurance company, and you, you're the babe in the woods. When you try to hustle a hustler, you are the one who's likely to come up short. Since it is difficult for a lay person to judge the quality of a body shop repair, you would do best to seek an honest deal from an honest shop and be happy to get what you've paid for, including the full deductible.

# Brake Failure
How to cope with a sudden loss

Brakes that fail let you know in one of two ways: either the pedal goes all the way to the floor with no effect, or the pedal feels rock hard and almost impossible to budge. The latter is the least serious; it signals a failure of the power brake booster, not the brakes themselves. If you push on the pedal with all your strength—use both feet if the pedal is wide enough—you should still be able to slow the car.

If the pedal sinks toward the floor with no resistance, there is probably a leak in the hydraulic system. The red BRAKE warning light on the dash will come on. On modern dual-circuit brake systems, half the brake system should still work, even if there is a leak in the other half. There are at least two types of dual-circuit brakes. On the most common, both front and both rear brakes are on separate circuits. On a diagonally-split system, each front brake is linked to the rear brake on the opposite side of the car.

The front brakes provide most of your stopping power. If they both fail, it will take a long distance to stop the car. Once you have stopped, call for a tow truck.

If one circuit of a diagonally-split system fails, you should notice some loss of stopping power and the car may pull to one side as you brake. Consider a tow if the car is difficult to drive.

If both rear brakes fail, you may hardly notice their loss, except for the warning light. You should be able to drive slowly and carefully to the nearest service station for repairs.

Check the level of brake fluid in the master cylinder (see BRAKE FLUID). If it's empty, add fluid and pump the brake pedal. Even if this seems to help, there will be air trapped in the brake lines. Have a mechanic bleed the air from the system and check for leaks as soon as possible.

Brakes sometimes fade due to overheating from hard use, such as descending a long series of hills. Stopping distance will increase dramatically. If the brakes fade, stop in a safe place for 15 or 20 minutes until they cool down; then drive cautiously in Low gear until you are sure the brakes are working.

If the brakes fail completely, pump the pedal—you may be able to build up pressure temporarily. Apply the parking (emergency) brake, but start gently and increase pressure gradually—slamming on the parking brake could throw you into a skid. Ease up on the parking brake immediately if the car begins to skid.

Begin shifting the car into lower gears, one at a time, and let the engine's drag slow the car. If your car has a manual transmission, ease the clutch in after shifting down—popping the clutch may lock the drive wheels and cause a skid. On automatic transmissions, be careful to shift down only one gear at a time, from DRIVE to SECOND, then FIRST, for example.

If all else fails, try to scrape the car along a guard rail, wall, hedge, or snow bank to slow it down. Running into dense shrubbery can stop a car if you are not going too fast.

# Brake Fluid
## How to make sure you've got enough

Hydraulic brake fluid is stored in a small reservoir under the hood. The reservoir is attached to the brake master cylinder and power booster. The power booster looks like an aluminum sauce pan, and is attached to the firewall between the engine and passenger compartments on the driver's side of the car.

Some reservoirs are translucent plastic; you can see the level of the fluid inside without removing the cap. If you do have to remove the cap, wipe it off first with a rag or paper towel so that no dirt gets into the reservoir. Round caps simply screw off; rectangular caps are usually held on by a heavy metal clip or a bolt.

Use a screwdriver to pry off the clip. Remove the cap and any rubber diaphragms underneath to check the fluid level. Fluid should be up to the FULL level marked on the reservoir or within a half an inch of the top. If the level is low, add fresh fluid from a new container.

Brake fluid is usually rated DOT 3 or DOT 4; check your Owner's Manual for the type recommended for your car. Since brake fluid can ruin paint, be careful not to spill it.

If the fluid level is frequently low, have a mechanic check the system for leaks. If one or both sections of the reservoir is empty, add fluid, replace the cap, and pump the brake pedal repeatedly. Check the level again and add more fluid if necessary. Then have a mechanic bleed any trapped air from the system. Air bubbles reduce the efficiency of the hydraulic system. Air can be forced out of the hydraulic lines by a process called "bleeding the brakes."

Brake fluid absorbs moisture, which can corrode parts of the system and cause the brakes to fade. Always cap a brake fluid container tightly, and never use fluid from an old, previously opened container. As a precaution, have a mechanic bleed the brakes and replace all the fluid every few years or whenever it becomes discolored.

## Brakes, Anti-lock
ABS to the rescue!

Anti-lock brake systems (ABS) are the greatest safety advance since seatbelts. Now offered on a number of models, ABS employs a computer to pump the brakes and help avoid skids (see SKID CONTROL). Here's how it works:

Speed sensors at each wheel or axle feed data to a computer that compares individual speeds of all four wheels. If one wheel decelerates more rapidly than the others, it's a sign that the wheel is about to skid. The computer then operates valves in the brake lines to momentarily reduce braking force at that wheel. In effect, the computer "pumps" the brakes for you, one or more wheels at a time as required.

The result is dramatic. On a slippery road, a car

with normal brakes will often skid straight ahead in a panic stop, its front wheels sliding rather than rolling, losing all steering control. A car equipped with ABS simply comes to a safe stop in the shortest possible distance while maintaining full steering control.

ABS will not, of course, repeal the laws of physics: if you enter a turn driving too fast for the road conditions, the car may still skid whether you have ABS or not.

The high price of ABS ($800 to $1500 at this writing) is expected to come down in time, bringing this life-saving option within reach of most car buyers.

# Breakdowns
## How to handle

If your car breaks down, turn on the emergency flashers immediately and try to coast off the road. If you can't get off the road, set up flares (if you have them), get out of the car, and wait well off the road.

If you have a CB radio, use it to call for help on Channel 9 (the emergency channel) or Channel 19 (the truckers' channel—see CB RADIO). Tie a white cloth to the door handle or radio antenna to signal other drivers that you need help. Ask all drivers who stop to phone the police or your auto club from the next phone booth, or to alert toll booth personnel.

If you're stuck in a familiar area within walking distance of a phone booth or service station, lock your car and walk for help. Keep well off a major highway. Walk on the side facing traffic if you are on a secondary road with no sidewalks. If you're stuck in a strange area, it may be best to stay inside the locked car and tie a white cloth to the door handle or antenna (see DRIVING ALONE).

If you think you can repair the problem yourself, see the TROUBLESHOOTING guides at the front of this book. If your car needs to be towed, see TOW TRUCKS.

# Bulb Replacement
Easy when you know how

There are a dozen or more light bulbs under plastic lenses on the outside of most cars, and sometimes even more on the inside: courtesy lights, dome light, glove compartment light, trunk light, etc. There may be several bulbs in a single exterior housing. For example, the tail light cluster often contains separate bulbs for the turn signal, brake light, backup light, and the tail light itself.

There are basically three ways to get at an exterior light bulb. If the lens has visible screws, remove the screws and lens, then remove the bulb by pushing it into its spring-loaded socket and turning it counter-clockwise about a quarter turn.

If the entire light housing comes off with the lens, the bulb and socket are usually removed from the back of the housing. Twist the socket to remove it, then remove the bulb by pushing and twisting.

Some sockets can be reached without removing the housing from the car body—check inside the trunk or behind the bumper or fender to see if you can remove the the unit.

Take the bad bulb along when you buy a replacement—you want to make sure the new bulb has the same model number. If you can find the model numbers in your owner's manual, buy some spares of each type to carry in the car.

To insert a new bulb, align the pins on the sides of

the bulb with the slots in the socket, then push in and twist clockwise to seat the bulb. Refit the socket or lens.

The white plastic lenses of dome and cargo lights inside the car are often removed by squeezing them gently or by pulling them straight off. Instrument panel lights are hard to reach and may require disassembly of the dash. Leave them to a pro.

## Buying a New Car
Getting the one that's right for you

Most people hate shopping for a car. That's because car dealers sometimes seem to have all the scruples of child pornographers. Salesmen work on commission, so they are more interested in selling the most expensive car and options they can unload than in helping you to select a car you'll be happy with in the long run. To make matters worse, few sales people know the products they sell. The only way to come out ahead is to do your homework and refuse to be manipulated.

Before you go anywhere near a car showroom, sit down with a pad and pencil and list the sort of things you *need* a car for, and the features it must therefore have. For example, do you need the car to commute? Do you commute alone or in a car pool? How many seats do you need—two? five? nine? Do you need to transport bulky items frequently—lumber, house-plants, horses? This list should help you to focus in on the kind of wheels you need, whether sports car or station wagon, pickup truck or van, utility vehicle or sedan. If you need to tow a trailer, order the special trailer-towing package of heavy-duty equipment.

Now, make a second list of features you would *like* on your car, such as: transmission type (automatic or manual); air conditioning; power seats, windows, mirrors, etc.; sunroof; sound system (stereo, tape deck, CD player, etc.); two doors or four; a small, medium, or large-size car; and so on. Don't make any firm decision on engine size yet (four, six, or eight cylinders); this is academic until you begin test driving.

Once you know this much, you should be ready for your first trip to the showrooms. Take along your notepad, and make another list of the cars you see that meet your needs, the engines and options available on each one, and their list prices.

If "heavy-duty" parts are offered, such as the battery, suspension, or cooling system, this is a sign that the standard design is marginal, and you will want the heavy-duty parts. So-called "sport" suspension and high-performance tires can give you an important safety margin in an emergency; you don't have to be a race driver to order them.

Sit in the cars that interest you to see if the seats are comfortable, if you can easily reach all the controls, and if the car generally "fits" you well; if you are a typical buyer, you'll be living with your new car for five to seven years. Also, take a good look at the trunk space.

Don't go for a test drive at this point, let alone sign anything. And don't let the sales person confuse you with talk about how, "I can put you into this baby for X dollars a month." Say that you're still comparison shopping, and will be back later if this car is still in the running. But do ask about all the options available on the cars you're interested in, and get their prices.

In the quiet of your home, go over your lists and start to eliminate cars. Set your absolute price limit for cars and options, and eliminate any that are more than 20% over your limit (you're not likely to get more than 20% off the list price, even if you are a good haggler). Drop cars that are not available in the body style you want. Cross off those unavailable with the options you want or need. Eliminate cars you cannot find at local dealers. Knock off cars with poor reliability records or that have recall histories that make you uneasy. Throw out any cars that didn't "fit" you.

With any luck, your list will now have six cars or fewer to drive. Before you get to each dealership, pick out a test route that includes residential streets and a short stretch of high-speed highway, hills and curves, smooth and rough pavement. Insist on driving a car equipped the way you want to buy it. Make a list of the following items for each car, rating them on a scale of one to five: seat comfort; visibility in all directions; engine starting; engine smoothness; control convenience; transmission shifting; acceleration; steering; braking; maneuverability; ride comfort; handling stability; noise level; ventilation; and the all-important sound system.

You can ask for the dealer's best price now, but don't sign anything until you've gone home and compared your scorecards for the different cars. If one model stands out way ahead of the rest, all that's left is bargaining over the price. If several models are close, you may be able to play one dealer off against another.

Before you talk price seriously, find out the dealer's cost for the basic car and its options in newsstand price guides or consumer magazines. As a general rule, the dealer's cost for a small car is about 87% of the sticker price; on stripped base models dealer cost can run to 93%, which is why dealers hate to sell these models. Dealer cost on compacts is about 86%. Midsize cars cost the dealer 85% of list price. Large cars cost the dealer about 84% of list price. Options have an average cost of 85%. The destination (shipping) charge listed on the sticker has no markup and is nonnegotiable. Calculate the cost for the car and all options, then add the destination charge for the total dealer cost.

A good haggler should be able to buy a car for $300 to $500 over the dealer's cost. Most buyers will pay twice that, so a dealer can afford to let the occasional car go for less...after some hard bargaining. You will often hear this popular opening line: "How much will you give me for this baby." That's when to hit them with your $200-over-cost quote, and haggle up reluctantly, especially if you have other candidates on your list.

The salesman will cry and moan over this offer, but you must remember that the dealer's actual cost is lower than any invoice, or "tissue," the sales person may show you. Most car companies hold back three percent of the car's cost, and refund it to the dealer after the car has been sold. This gives the dealer an extra $200 to $800 profit, even on a car apparently selling for "cost."

Some dealers demand more than sticker price for popular models in short supply, or else pack them with unwanted options. It is always a bad idea to pay more than list price, because the resale value of an overpriced car will not hold up in the long run. Always refuse to pay for dealer- or distributor-installed options you don't want, or for markups listed on a separate sticker next to the manufacturer's sticker.

Try not to confuse your price negotiations with a trade-in; that gives sales people too many variables to juggle. They may cut you a great deal on the new car price while robbing you blind on your trade-in. You'll generally get a higher price by selling your old car privately.

Remember that no price is final until the sales manager approves the deal and signs the order form. Beware of the "good cop/bad cop" routine in which the friendly sales person says that the mean old sales manager "won't let me sell it for less than X dollars." If the bottom line is out of line, shop elsewhere.

Don't be ashamed to read all of the fine print in the contract and ask to have any objectionable clauses removed. Make sure the agreement says you can get your deposit back if the deal falls through (if the car is not delivered by the promised date, for example).

The order form is a legal contract that should specify the car's color and all the optional equipment you have ordered, the delivery date, and the total price, including all taxes, shipping charges and dealer prep fees. You can refuse to accept delivery of a car with options you didn't order, including dealer-applied rust-proofing and expensive protective finishes for upholstery and paint. If you do, the dealer will often throw them in for free.

The contract usually gives the dealer the right to change the price if the factory raises its prices before the car is delivered. Make sure it also gives you the right to cancel if the new price is too high for you.

You should shop for financing as carefully as you do for the car (see LOANS).

# Buying a Used Car
## How not to get stuck

Used cars can be a great bargain or a total waste of money, depending on your luck and knowledge of cars. You can improve your chances by first determining the kind of car you need (see BUYING A NEW CAR, above). Small to medium sedans are generally the best buy. Luxury models and convertibles are expensive even secondhand, and are loaded with troublesome power equipment. Performance cars tend to be abused and expensive to keep in tune.

Check the frequency-of-repair information printed in the April and December issues of *Consumer Reports*, available in most libraries. Once you have narrowed your list to a few models, look up their retail and wholesale values in one of the used car price guides found on newsstands or in the *NADA Official Used Car Guide*, found in some libraries and banks. Now you are ready to do some serious shopping.

The best (and worst) used cars are sold by individual car owners. Private owners usually will accept close to the wholesale price, but they provide no guarantee. Try to buy a car whose history you know, preferably from a trusted friend, relative, or co-worker.

New car dealers often have the best, newest, and most expensive used cars, for they generally keep only the best trade-ins and auction off the lemons. (They also may buy cars at auction. Always ask the dealer for the car's service history, and be suspicious of cars a dealer isn't familiar with.) Any warranty should cover both parts and labor. Since the markup on used cars is greater than on new ones, their prices are highly negotiable.

Used car dealers run the gamut from respected establishments to fly-by-night "gypsies." Their prices should be lower than a new car dealer's, but many have limited service facilities and skimpy warranties. Most of their cars are bought at auctions.

Avoid cars being sold by rental companies or other fleets. Such cars are often abused and many receive hit-or-miss maintenance. Even their highly touted one-year warranties are less generous than the transferable part of the five- to seven-year warranty on late-model cars that were originally bought by a private party.

Inspect a used car in fair weather during the day, as rain and darkness can mask many defects. Check the bodywork for rust or signs of accident repairs. Operate all windows, doors, hood, and trunk to check for binding or misalignment caused by accidents. Check tires for uneven wear, which may signal a bent chassis. Inspect the underside for leaking coolant, oil, brake, or transmission fluid.

Check under the hood for proper coolant, oil, battery, brake, and transmission fluid levels. Low levels indicate spotty maintenance. Metal particles, foam, or sludge on the oil dipstick are signs of serious engine trouble. Automatic transmission fluid with a burned smell or milky deposits signal problems in the transmission.

Inspect the interior for wear or damage. Water marks, rust, musty odor, and sand or mud under carpets and seats are signs of flood damage—and electrical connections that will soon corrode.

When you have found a car that passes this inspection, take it for a test drive, as described in BUYING A NEW CAR. Try all the power accessories to make sure they work. Have a partner check all exterior lights and signals. Make sure none of the wheels wobble, that the exhaust doesn't smoke, and that the car travels in a straight line, (not slightly skewed, which indicates a bent chassis or suspension).

Try the transmission in all gears, including REVERSE. Slipping, noise, or jerky shifts indicate expensive work.

Brakes should stop the car smoothly and in a straight line at high and low speeds without grabbing, pulling to one side, or making noise. Try the parking brake on a hill.

Note how the car steers and handles. There should be less than two inches of free play in the wheel and no noise, looseness, shimmy, or vagueness in the steering.

Listen for squeaks or rattles. At the end of the drive, check again for fluid leaks. Then try to restart the hot engine; it should start smoothly.

If the car passes all these tests, take it to your mechanic for a thorough test. Ask him to inspect brakes, suspension, and steering, and to do a compression test on the engine and a converter stall test on the transmission. Get a written estimate for any work needed, and ask the seller to deduct that amount from the price. Also phone the NHTSA hotline (800-424-9393) to see if that make and model was the subject of a recall. If it was, ask the seller for proof that the car was fixed.

When buying from a private party or a dealer who doesn't know the car's history, it's a good idea to write down the Vehicle Identification Number (found on the dash, near the windshield) and ask the police to run a stolen car check on it. The police can seize a stolen car at any time and return it to its rightful owner, leaving you to sue a seller who may have fled.

If you buy the car, get a formal bill of sale stating the make, model, and year of the car, the vehicle I.D. number, the mileage on the odometer, the name and address of both buyer and seller, and the sale price. Make sure you have the title or registration signed over to you.

After that, you've done all you can (save crossing your fingers) to avoid getting stuck.

# Car Companies
Addresses of their presidents

When filing a complaint about a car (see ARBITRA-TION, COMPLAINTS, CONSUMER ADVOCATES, LEMON LAWS, and WARRANTIES), it is sometimes satisfying to fire off a strong letter to the company president. This is seldom effective, however, because few executives open their own mail. Secretaries screen the mail for complaints and shuttle them over to the consumer affairs department (which you should have written to first). If you write a brief letter on fancy stationery, hand address the envelope, mark it "Personal and Confidential," and perhaps scent it lightly with perfume, it has a better chance of getting to the top. What secretary would dare to open and read it?

Because the tenure of auto executives is volatile, give the car company a call to check for last-minute title or name changes. The number should be in your owner's manual.

Here are the people to write to at each company:

Joseph Greco, President and CEO, **Alfa Romeo** Inc., 250 Sylvan Ave., Englewood Cliffs, NJ 07632.

**American Motors/Jeep/Renault**: see Chrysler, below.

Michael Haysey, Director of Marketing, **Aston Martin Lagonda** of North America, Inc., 180 Harvard Ave., Stamford, CT 06902.

Michael Jackling, Executive Vice President, **BMW** of North America, BMW Plaza, Montvale, NJ 07645.

Lee Iacocca, Chairman, **Chrysler** Corp., P.O. Box 1919, Detroit, MI 48121.

Donald Petersen, Chairman, **Ford** Motor Co., The

American Rd., Dearborn, MI 48121.

Roger Smith, Chairman, **General Motors** Corp., GMC Bldg., Detroit, MI 48202.

Tetsuo Chino, President, American **Honda** Motor Co. [including **Acura**], 100 W. Alondra Blvd., Gardena, CA 90247.

Max Jamiesson, Exec. VP, **Hyundai** Motor America, 7373 Hunt Ave., Garden Grove, CA 92642.

Masashi Suzuki, President, American **Isuzu** Motors, 2300 Pellissier Place, Whittier, CA 90601.

Graham Whitehead, President, **Jaguar** Cars Inc., 600 Willow Tree Rd., Leonia, NJ 07605.

Wesley Fredericks, Chairman, **Lotus** Performance Cars, 530 Walnut St., Norwood, NJ 07648.

Hisao Kaide, President, **Mazda** of North America, 1444 McGraw Ave., Irvine, CA 92714.

Erich Krampe, President, **Mercedes-Benz** of North America, One Mercedes Dr., Montvale, NJ 07645.

Kazue Naganuma, Chairman, **Mitsubishi** of America, 1054 Talbert St., Fountain Valley, CA 92708.

Kazutoshi Hagiwara, President, **Nissan** Motor Corp., 18501 Figueroa St., Carson, CA 90248.

Pascal Henault, President, **Peugeot** Motors of America, One Peugeot Plaza, Lyndhurst, NJ 07071.

John Cook, President, **Porsche** Cars of North America, 200 S. Virginia, St., Reno, NV 89501.

Charles Hughes, President, **Range Rover** of North America, P.O. Box 1503, Lanham, MD 20706.

Robert Schwartz, President, **Rolls Royce** Motors Inc., P.O. Box 476, Lyndhurst, NJ 07071.

Robert Sinclair, President, **Saab**-Scania of America, Saab Dr., Orange, CT 06477.

Norman Braman, Chairman, ARCONA [**Sterling**], 8325 NW 53rd St., Miami, FL 33166.

Harvey Lamm, Chairman, **Subaru** of America, P.O.

Box 6000, Cherry Hill, NJ 08034-6000.

Yuki Togo, President, **Toyota** Motor Sales USA, 19001 S. Western Ave., Torrance, CA 90509.

Noel Phillips, Chief Executive Officer, **Volkswagen** of America (including **Audi**), 888 W. Big Beaver Rd., Troy, MI 48099.

Joseph Nicolato, Chairman, **Volvo** Cars of North America, One Volvo Dr., Rockleigh, NJ 07647.

Malcolm Bricklin, Chairman, **Yugo** America Inc., 28 Park Way, Upper Saddle River, NJ 07458.

# Carpet
## How to clean and repair

Vacuum carpeting often to remove abrasive sand and dirt, which can wear it out, especially under the pedals and in other high-use areas. Remove the floor mats to clean them, and vacuum under them. If you don't have floormats, you can get them in auto parts and department stores—they are good protection.

Special carpet cleaners are also sold in auto parts stores. Household cleaners may not be effective because of fire-retarding chemicals used in auto carpeting. For problem stains, see the cleaning instructions for UPHOLSTERY.

To repair cigarette burns, cut away charred strands with curved cuticle scissors. Cut replacement loops from a section of good carpet under the seats or in another hidden spot. Glue the replacement loops into the damaged area with a clear-drying waterproof glue. (White household or carpenter's glue is not waterproof; try model cement.)

# Catalytic Converter
## Cleaning up your act

The three-way catalytic converter built into the exhaust system of most modern cars is the most effective of many anti-pollution devices. This is a stainless steel chamber that looks like a muffler and is spliced into the exhaust system. Inside the catalytic converter is a ceramic honeycomb or beads coated with three rare metals: platinum, rhodium, and palladium. In the presence of sufficient oxygen, these metals act as catalysts to change three pollutants—carbon monoxide, nitrogen oxides, and hydrocarbons—into harmless carbon dioxide, nitrogen, and water vapor.

Older cars have a simpler oxidation catalyst filled with platinum-coated ceramic. It converts hydrocarbons and carbon monoxide into water vapor and carbon dioxide.

The catalyst on a new car will sometimes emit a rotten egg odor. There are chemicals, sold in auto parts stores, that you can add to the gas to reduce this odor, but this is usually a sign that the air-fuel ratio is wrong or that the catalyst is improperly designed. Ask your dealer if there is a factory repair listed in a TSB (see TECHNICAL SERVICE BULLETINS).

All cars with catalysts must run on unleaded gas. Using leaded gas can ruin the catalyst and cause it to overheat and fuse, which will block the exhaust system, and even melt asphalt or set dry leaves afire under the car. Some unethical firms still sell "test pipes" to replace the catalytic converter with a useless hollow pipe. These not only allow pollution, but may disrupt the operation of today's delicately balanced computer-controlled fuel systems, which depend on a certain amount of backpressure in the exhaust system.

By federal law, catalytic converters must be guaranteed by the car maker for five years or 50,000 miles, provided you use lead-free gas (see WARRANTIES). Sooner or later, however, the catalyst will rust out, become blocked, or otherwise fail. Replacing it can be expensive, but is necessary. A factory replacement should last another five years or 50,000 miles, but it can cost $300 to $500—a lot of money to spend on an older car. If you don't intend to keep your car that long, you can get a smaller replacement catalyst for $100 to $150 or so. Make sure the replacement catalyst has a certification label from the Environmental Protection Agency.

# Cats
## How to transport safely

A loose cat in a car can be as hazardous as a loose cannon on a ship. Startled by sudden movement or noise, even a normally friendly feline may panic and claw the driver, tear upholstery, soil carpeting, leap from an open window, or otherwise ruin a pleasant drive.

A cat should always be placed in a carrier box before you take the animal out of the house. Use a carrier specifically designed for cats, with adequate ventilation and a securely locking top. Use the seatbelt to keep the carrier from rolling or falling should you make a sudden stop.

A nervous cat may be more comfortable if the carrier vents are positioned so the animal can see its owner. Never place the carrier in the trunk, no matter how noisy or obnoxious the cat becomes—exhaust gasses may leak into the trunk and kill or permanently brain damage the animal.

Never leave any animal (or infant, for that matter) locked in a parked car. Even with the windows open slightly for ventilation, temperatures in a parked car can reach alarming heights, causing heat prostration or cardiac arrest.

## Cassette Tapes
### Cleaning and unjamming

A malfunctioning tape player will sometimes snag a tape and pull it out of the cassette. To rewind it, first lay the tape on a flat surface and press out any wrinkles with your fingernail. Press a tapered cap from a marker or pen into one of the reels on the cassette and twist it to wind the tape back into the cassette. If the tape is broken, you can get a splicing kit from an electronics supply store such as Radio Shack.

If the tape is jammed and twisted inside the cassette, gently fish it out with a paper clip bent into a hook. Then press out any wrinkles and rewind. To prevent your tapes from getting "eaten," keep them tightly wound and in their individual cases.

Clean the tape heads inside the cassette player periodically to remove oxide buildup. This will make your tapes sound better and last longer. There are two types of cleaning cassettes that do the job automatically when you run them through the player. Cleaning cassettes to which you add a liquid cleaning solution are the safest. They work well if you use them frequently (every few weeks). Dry cleaners are abrasive and can cause the recording heads to wear, but they may be needed if there is a substantial oxide buildup on heads that haven't been cleaned for months or years.

Never leave cassettes in the hot sun on dashboards or seats; the tape may be damaged. Keep them out of sight in the glove compartment, console, or special cassette cases. Don't play tapes in cold weather until you have had a chance to warm up the passenger compartment; cassette players are more likely to damage cold cassettes than warm ones.

# CB Radio
## The good buddy network

The fad for Citizen's Band (CB) radio has pretty much faded, freeing up airwaves previously clogged by morons with fake southern accents pretending to be good ol' boy truckers. This is a good thing, because CB radio can be a useful tool for emergencies or everyday commuting.

A modern CB transceiver [transmitter-receiver] is a two-way radio with 40 channels. State police monitor Channel 9, which should be used only for emergency broadcasts. Many truckers use channel 19, which can be a good source of traffic information, tips on radar traps, and other useful advice, if you can understand what they're saying and stand the way they say it. Despite an FCC ban on profanity, no one blips CB radio!

Everyone broadcasting on CB is supposed to use a "handle" or nickname, which is how you can identify regular commuters. Every CB channel is a party line, so you can just listen in for useful information or add to the chatter. If you want to break into a conversation, you're supposed to say: "Breaker..." and the channel number. For example: "Breaker One Nine," will break into channel 19.

If you are having a conversation that is repeatedly interrupted, ask the person you are speaking with to switch to another channel. Pick one at random to see if it's less crowded.

In an emergency, dial channel 9, depress the push-to-talk button, and state that there is an emergency. Release the button and listen for a reply. When you get the police or another CB'er who can relay your message, state the nature of your problem and your location, such as a route number and the number on the nearest mile marker. If you get no response, keep switching channels until you hear a conversation, then break into it and ask for help. The range of CB radio is only a few miles; your message may have to be relayed by several cooperative CB'ers to reach the closest trooper.

Be aware that not all CB listeners are good buddies. Some criminals and perverts monitor the airwaves looking for victims. After someone answers your call for help, try again on another channel and ask a second person to telephone the police, just to make sure.

CB radios used to be permanently installed, but

they were often stolen from parked cars. You can now buy portable models with magnetic antennas that stick to the roof. When you park, you can lock a portable CB in the trunk or take it with you.

## Child Seats
How to choose and use them

Auto accidents are the leading cause of death and serious injury to children. Reportedly, almost 80% of these deaths could be avoided by the proper use of an approved child safety seat. All 50 states now require the use of safety seats for children of varying ages. Your state police or motor vehicle bureau can tell you the requirements in your state. And, of course, wearing your own safety belt will set a good example for the child.

Many designs are available for infants or children of different ages. Infant seats are designed for babies who are not old enough to sit up by themselves. They make handy infant carriers that you can take into stores and use around the house. Child seats are for older children (up to five years old; after age five, children can begin to use adult lap belts).

All seats are held in place by the car's safety belt. The safest position for these is in the center of the rear seat, if the seatbelts reel in and out of the space between the seat back and cushion. If the belts reel out of a slot in the cushion forward of the seat back, a child seat may not be properly anchored.

Some child seats require an additional tether strap that must go over the car's seat back and be bolted to the rear package shelf or cargo floor. Although tethered seats are the most stable, the vast majority are installed improperly, so they're best avoided in favor of seats that are easier to install.

Children are not only safer, but are often better behaved when restrained in a safety seat. For one thing, the seat is elevated so the child can see out of the car, and stay amused for longer periods of time.

There are many brands and types of safety seat on the market. They can be ordered through the parts departments of some new car dealers, or bought in department or children's stores. Thanks to federal regulations, they are all safer than no restraint at all. However, some models are more convenient and comfortable than others.

Try a seat before you buy it—or at least make sure you can return it if you are not satisfied. A seat that is easy to install and use will probably be used more often. Cover the seat with a light-colored blanket or towel when the car is parked so it won't overheat in the sun. Little buns don't like hot seats any more than big ones.

## Children
Tips for travelling

Keeping children amused on a long trip is an art. Children are singularly unimpressed by scenery, architecture and/or fine restaurants. When travelling with kids, a good rule of thumb for restaurants is: no place nice and no place twice.

Younger children can often be kept occupied with favorite books or toys. But keeping lots of them aboard is not only messy, it can be a safety hazard if an accident or short stop sends them flying. One good idea is to attach a shoe caddy to the back of a front seat where you can store toys and soft-covered books in the pouches.

Portable video games are popular with older children, but be sure to use only those equipped with a "mute" switch—several hundred miles of video beeps and blips can be unnerving.

Radios or tape decks with headphones let kids listen to their favorite music without inflicting it upon you.

Frequent stops are a must, especially for little bladders. Children confined to safety seats need periodic release to restore circulation. Always carry an ample supply of paper towels and tissues for emergencies.

Children who are prone to car sickness may feel less queasy in the front seat than in the rear.

## Complaints
How to get satisfaction on repairs

Every time the government does a survey on consumer complaints, car repairs far surpass every other category. To get results, there's a definite order in which complaints should be made. Keep a careful log of your problem, with dates and receipts. Also, make photocopies of bills, dealer service orders, written repair estimates, and any complaint letters you send. If you follow the steps listed below, you will be preparing the proper groundwork for arbitration, lemon law procedures, or even a lawsuit, if it comes to that.

1) If you are not satisfied with any repair work, bring the car back to the shop, along with a list of uncorrected trouble. Make a copy of the list for your log. If the unsatisfactory work was done at a new car dealership, talk to the service manager (not to the service writers, who are just repair sales people on commission). If the problem is not obvious, ask to have the mechanic who will be working on the car go for a short test drive so that he can evaluate the problem.

2) If several attempts do not cure the problem, get a second opinion in writing from an independent mechanic you know to be competent. If your car is under warranty, do not have an independent mechanic work on it—you may not be reimbursed by the car maker. Bring the written estimate to the original car dealership and have them try the repair suggested by your independent mechanic. If the car is under warranty, see WARRANTIES to find out how to proceed at this point.

3) If the shop still cannot fix the problem, ask for a refund or adjustment on any unsuccessful work that you've already paid for. If you cannot get satisfaction, file a complaint with the local Better Business Bureau and ask them to mediate the problem. (Also, see ARBITRATION.) Or contact your local "action line" newspaper, radio, or TV reporter, and send a copy of your complaint to the garage. Also contact the state Attor-

ney General's office (c/o your state capital), and any state mechanic licensing office.

4) Always pay for repair work by credit card, if possible. In the case of a repair dispute for $50 or more in your home state, you may withhold the disputed amount from your credit card payments. The amount will be charged back to the repair shop. If the shop wants to fight the chargeback, they will have to go to court. To initiate a chargeback, write to the credit card company, submit copies of your log and other paperwork, state that negotiations with the mechanic have broken down, and use the magic words, "chargeback" and "Fair Credit Billing Act of 1975." Ask that the disputed amount be credited to your account.

5) As a last resort, take your case to court. You won't need a lawyer if your case qualifies for small claims court. There is a limit, however, to the dollar amount of a dispute that the small claims court will hear; if your bill is more than that amount, you will need a lawyer (see LAWYERS).

# Computers
## Self-diagnostic technology

Most modern car engines are computer-controlled. They use sophisticated microprocessors to control the engine's operation, rather than the mechanical controls of older cars. This is usually more of a blessing than a curse.

Although the computer is often blamed for any problem a mechanic can't solve, car makers say that the vast majority of computers returned to them for warranty credit are working just fine. Like a digital wristwatch or pocket calculator, if the computer works fine for the first few weeks, it will probably work forever.

Many computers have a self-diagnostic circuit that can spot problems and store trouble codes in its memory. The mechanic can read these codes to find out what's wrong with the engine. And you can use them to check up on both your car and the mechanic. Most computers will let you know when they have stored a trouble code by a warning light on the dash that says CHECK ENGINE or SERVICE ENGINE SOON.

On some cars the trouble codes are easy to trigger. On a few Cadillacs, for instance, if you press the OFF and WARM buttons on the climate control simultaneously, a code number will appear on the digital temperature display. Other cars require fiddling under the dash or hood. Instructions for triggering and interpreting trouble codes appear in the factory shop manual, which is available for about $25 to $50 from the dealer's parts department. Many other repair manuals used by independent shops also list these codes. If you have a good relationship with the dealer's service manager or an independent mechanic, they may let you copy down the trouble codes for your car from their manuals.

## Consumer Groups
Help when you need it most

A number of groups provide help to individuals battling over warranty, safety, or repair problems. Some of these groups are government agencies, others are industry associations or non-profit groups that have been organized to help frustrated consumers. Here are their addresses and the kinds of problems they tackle:

**Auto Protection Association**, 292 ouest, boul. St. Joseph, Montreal, Quebec H2V 2N7; phone (514) 273-1366; or 7 Dundas Sq., Suite 302, Toronto, Ontario M5B 1B5; phone (416) 367-2595. Handles Canadian consumer complaints.

**Center for Auto Safety**, 2001 S St. NW, Washington, DC 20009; phone (202) 328-7700. Deals with safety, warranty and recall problems. The Center also has a list of lawyers who specialize in auto repair complaints. A self-addressed, business-size envelope with 2 oz. postage will assure priority treatment by this non-profit organization.

**Council of Better Business Bureaus**, Automotive Programs, Suite 600, 1515 Wilson Blvd., Arlington, VA 22209; phone (703) 276-0100. Will refer you to local BBBs that mediate or arbitrate general consumer complaints, including deceptive sales practices, ineffective repairs to new or used cars, warranty disputes, and other abuses. Before contacting CBBB, see your Yellow Pages for your local BBB.

**Environmental Protection Agency**, 401 M St. SW, Washington, DC 20460; phone (202) 382-2090. Sets and enforces air and noise pollution standards for cars and trucks; also measures fuel economy. May assist in 50,000-mile pollution control equipment warranty disputes. Publishes official *EPA Gas Mileage Guide*.

**Federal Trade Commission**, Bureau of Consumer Protection, Pennsylvania Ave. at 6th St. NW, Washington, DC 20580. Investigates deceptive advertising and credit practices in auto sales and repairs. Phone (202) 326-3153 for Deceptive Advertising Division; (202) 326-3225 for Deceptive Credit Practices Division.

**National Automobile Dealers Association**, AUTOCAP Program, 8400 Westpark Dr., McLean, VA 22102; phone (703) 821-7144. Will refer you to local offices that administer mediation programs between dealers and buyers of some brands of cars.

**National Highway Traffic Safety Administration**, 400 7th St. SW, Washington, DC 20590; phone (800) 424-9393. In the D.C. metro area, phone 366-0123. Compiles data on safety defects, orders recalls, supplies information on past recalls of individual cars, has files of safety-related technical service bulletins, supplies safety-related literature on request, and can refer you to the correct government agency for other problems.

# D

## De-icing Windows

Keeping a weather eye on the road

Windshield and rear window defrosters take time to work, and may not clear thick accumulations of ice. Clear frost from all windows (front, sides and rear) before driving. It is dangerous to drive with just a few peep holes scratched into the frost.

Aerosol de-icers make fast work of this job, but many contain alcohol, which can damage rubber weatherstripping around the windows. Alcohol will also cool the glass as it evaporates, causing moisture in the air to re-freeze. Turn you car defrosters on HIGH to warm the glass before applying the aerosol.

Always carry a plastic ice scraper in the car in winter. If you are caught without one, use a stiff edge—such as a credit card—to scrape away ice.

To prevent ice from sticking to the windshield, cover it in the evening with strong plastic; a heavy-duty trash bag slit along two edges and opened flat works fine. Place the plastic over the windshield, covering the wipers. Close the car doors over the edges of the bag to hold it snug.

When you return to the car, sweep away heavy snow, then peel off the plastic and the ice will come with it. Ice that forms under the plastic will be clear enough to see through, and you can be driving while the defroster melts it.

An expensive alternative is a remote-control starter, which costs over $200 but can start your engine from inside the house while you have that final cup of coffee. If you set the defroster controls on *High* the night before, you can walk out to a toasty warm car with clear windows.

## Deodorizing Your Car
Getting the smell out of there

Foul odors can permeate cloth upholstery and headliners. Deodorizers sold by car washes and auto parts stores try to mask bad odors with strong perfume, which can be just as objectionable. Old household remedies are often the best. Keep the windows open whenever possible to air out the car. Empty ashtrays often. When windows must be closed, an open box of baking soda will absorb odors. Lemon juice or commercial sprays can neutralize fishy odors.

Concentrated deodorizers are sold in tiny bottles in pharmacies, hardware, and pet stores. They are used a few drops at a time to destroy strong odors, rather than covering them up. Do not confuse this with "Pimp Oil," a strong perfume sold in car washes.

A musty smell is a sign of water leaks that should

be fixed (see LEAKS). A rotten egg smell may come from the car's catalytic converter. This may be a symptom of an incorrect air/fuel mixture in the engine, or a faulty catalyst, which is covered by a 50,000-mile warranty. See your dealer or a good repair shop.

# Detailing
The ultimate wax job

Detailing is the name given to ultra-fussy wash-and-wax jobs done by professionals who go over the car (and often the engine) with toothbrushes and Q-Tips, if not a fine-toothed comb. Detailing is growing in popularity, and will make your car look like it's ready for an auto show, but it can cost from $40 to well over $300. If you decide your car deserves the very best, check out the detailing shop to be sure they're not using gasoline, shoe polish, or other potentially harmful products on the tender parts of the cars they clean.

# Dogs
## Cures for car chasers

Car chasing is not only dangerous for the dog, but a hazard to the driver and bystanders. Keeping the dog leashed or confined is the obvious solution, but not always practical or possible. If traditional obedience training fails to break this habit, enlist friends for a more radical approach.

Using a strange car, have someone sit in the back seat with a bucket of cold water and both windows open. Drive by your home when the dog is outside. Douse the dog with water if it chases the car. One or two "treatments" will usually break the dog of its habit. Use a different car each time, so the dog associates discomfort with the activity, not a particular car.

## How to transport dogs safely

Most dogs love to bound about in a car and stick their heads out the window. This is not only distracting to the driver, but hazardous to the dog. Dust in the air can cause serious eye damage when it hits the dog at highway speeds. An unrestrained dog can take a painful spill if the car stops short or corners too fast. It can also jostle the driver and cause a loss of control.

Small dogs should be transported in pet carriers (see CATS). Harnesses are available to restrain small to medium-sized dogs with the car's seatbelts. Large dogs should be confined to the back of a car or station wagon with a metal grille sold in pet shops.

On long trips, don't feed the dog for several hours before leaving. Stop frequently so the dog can relieve itself, and bring along a supply of fresh water and a dish to prevent dehydration.

Never leave an animal in a parked car for any length of time. Even if the windows are opened slightly for ventilation, temperatures inside the car can soar, leading to heat prostration or cardiac arrest. Leash the dog outside the car, or don't bring it along in the first place.

# Driving Alone
## Avoiding unwanted company

Driving by yourself, whether around town or coast-to-coast, is no big deal for tough guys like Clint Eastwood or Tom Selleck; but it certainly can be intimidating to the rest of us mortals, particularly women and senior citizens, who are often singled out by muggers.

To avoid problems, keep your car in good repair so it will be less likely to break down and put you at the mercy of passersby. Giving rides to hitch hikers or other strangers is really asking for trouble (see ASSAULTS).

Try to park in well-lit areas, away from vans and other large vehicles, which can provide a hiding place for crooks. Always lock the car and set the burglar alarm (if you have one). If you are a woman travelling alone, leave a man's hat in the car when you park it; potential thieves will assume the car belongs to a man and may pass it by.

When you return to a parked car, walk down the center of parking lot aisles, and look for suspicious characters hanging around the car or hiding behind other parked cars. You can create an emergency weapon by making a fist and placing keys between your fingers like the spikes on brass knuckles. Check the back seat and floor before you open the car—a break-in artist may be hiding there. If you see any of the above, get away from the car fast and phone the police.

When entering the car, get in fast and immediately lock the door behind you. If you have power door locks, unlock only the driver's door when you enter or leave the car; if you unlock all the doors at once, you may find that you have unexpected company.

If someone attacks you inside the car and you can't get out, beep the horn to attract attention, and trigger your burglar alarm (see THEFT ALARMS). If someone tries to enter the car while you are in it, drive off immediately, even if you have to run a red light or break another traffic law, so long as you can do so without triggering an accident.

If you're driving alone and another car bumps you gently from behind at a stop sign or light in a dangerous or lonely area, just ignore it. These "love taps" may be a sneaky way to get you out of your car. Just keep driving and check for damage when you get home.

If your car breaks down on a lonely highway or in a bad neighborhood, don't leave the car. Open the window once to tie a white handkerchief or cloth to the radio antenna or driver's door handle—the emergency "Help!" signal—then close the windows and keep them closed until the police or a tow truck arrives. If other drivers stop, open the window only enough to talk and ask them to phone the police for help. If you have a CB radio, use it to call for help (see CB RADIO).

## Drunk Driving
How to beat a bum rap

Drunk driving is no longer a laughing matter, thanks to the consciousness-raising activities of groups like MADD (Mothers Against Drunk Driving) and SADD (Students Against Drunk Driving). Fortunately, police and judges are cracking down on this offense as never before.

The best way to avoid trouble is to never drive after drinking any alcohol. The chart below (though an approximation) shows how little alcohol is required to raise blood levels to illegal levels. It's a good idea, when going to a party or dinner, to designate drivers who will not drink so they can safely drive others home. If you cannot find a volunteer to drive you home after drinking, call a friend, relative, or a taxi.

If the police stop you on suspicion of drunk driving, do not refuse a blood test; this can bring automatic penalties in most states. If you have been drinking and are involved in an accident, stay with your car—leaving the scene can lead to serious criminal charges.

Try to be polite and cooperative with police. If you

are arrested for Driving While Intoxicated (DWI) or Driving While Alcohol Impaired (DWAI), and feel that the charges are unjustified, consult a lawyer who specializes in DWI charges (see LAWYERS). Don't trust this one to the family attorney, who may not have experience in such matters.

## Drinking and Driving

How much alcohol can you drink and still drive safely? Preferably, none at all. But in most states you are not legally considered drunk unless you have a blood alcohol concentration (BAC) of 0.10% or higher. You can be charged with driving while alcohol impaired with a BAC of 0.05% to 0.09% in some states. Less than 0.05% means you are legally "sober." In actual fact, 0.05% will make most people light-headed; 0.10% is really blotto.

The chart below shows how few drinks are needed in a two-hour period to produce illegal BACs. (Note that the number of drinks depends on your weight.) A "drink" is considered one 4-oz. glass of wine, 1.2 oz. of 80-proof liquor, or 12 oz. of beer. This chart is only an estimate; different people have different tolerances for alcohol.

Source: New York State Dept. of Motor Vehicles

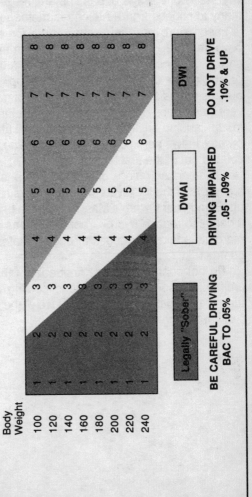

## Drinks (two-hour period)
### 1.2 oz. 80-Proof Liquor, 4 oz. Wine, or 12 oz. Beer

| Body Weight | | | | | | | | |
|---|---|---|---|---|---|---|---|---|
| 100 | 1 | 2 | 3 | 4 | 5 | 6 | 7 | 8 |
| 120 | 1 | 2 | 3 | 4 | 5 | 6 | 7 | 8 |
| 140 | 1 | 2 | 3 | 4 | 5 | 6 | 7 | 8 |
| 160 | 1 | 2 | 3 | 4 | 5 | 6 | 7 | 8 |
| 180 | 1 | 2 | 3 | 4 | 5 | 6 | 7 | 8 |
| 200 | 1 | 2 | 3 | 4 | 5 | 6 | 7 | 8 |
| 220 | 1 | 2 | 3 | 4 | 5 | 6 | 7 | 8 |
| 240 | 1 | 2 | 3 | 4 | 5 | 6 | 7 | 8 |

Legally "Sober"
BE CAREFUL DRIVING
BAC TO .05%

DWAI
DRIVING IMPAIRED
.05 - .09%

DWI
DO NOT DRIVE
.10% & UP

# Dry Gas
## When, why, and how to use it

DryGas is one brand of gas line antifreeze (there are many to choose from). A blend of methanol alcohol, it is used to prevent fuel system icing. On cold, damp days, moisture in gasoline can freeze in the fuel line, carburetor, or injection system, causing rough running or stalling before the engine warms up. Adding 12 ounces of this antifreeze to 10 gallons of gas can prevent freeze-up. However, if the carburetor is already frozen, adding antifreeze won't help until after the carburetor thaws out and the treated gasoline can be circulated out of the fuel tank.

High concentrations of methanol alcohol can damage parts of the fuel system in some cars (see GASOLINE and your Owner's Manual). On the brighter side, it can also reduce hydrocarbon emissions and help a marginal engine to squeak through a state emissions control test.

Do not confuse gas line antifreeze with the glycol antifreeze used in radiators and cooling systems—they are two different chemicals. Use of the wrong one can cause engine damage.

# E

## Emergency Road Service
### Calling out the cavalry

The AAA is the oldest and best-known organization offering 24-hour emergency road service to its members, but many oil companies, car makers, and other firms offer similar plans. Surveys show that drivers use these services for the following reasons: almost 50% use them for cars that won't start (often because of a dead battery); nearly 33% for breakdowns that require towing; 10% to change flats (or repair a flat and inflate a spare that didn't have any air!); 3% for keys locked in the car; and 2% for cars that have run out of gas. While the majority of these problems can be avoided with conscientious maintenance, it's still nice to know you have a reliable backup, should you need it.

The provisions of different plans vary greatly. Check all the fine print in the membership application before you sign up. Some plans are offered free of charge for several years when you purchase a new car. At this writing, Volvo offers membership in the Amoco Motor Club (with several exclusive extras) for three years when you buy a new Volvo. Peugeot offers free AAA membership. Hyundai, Jaguar, Nissan, and Sterling currently offer free road service plans to buyers through the Cross Country Motor Club. Most Mercedes-Benz dealers participate in a plan that will dispatch a dealership mechanic in a specially-equipped station wagon when you call for help.

For a modest annual membership fee, motor clubs provide a tow truck or mechanic when members call a toll-free emergency number. The service or tow may be free, discounted, or reimbursed later (up to certain limits), depending on the provisions of your plan. Many include such extra features as: personalized trip planning and maps; discount coupons for hotels, restaurants, rental cars, and popular tourist attractions; rewards for recovery of your car if it is stolen; emergency check cashing privileges; guaranteed arrest bond; accident insurance; limited reimbursement of legal defense fees (for traffic violations), food and lodging costs (if your car is disabled in an accident), and air fare for the entire family if your car breaks down on a vacation trip and you are forced to fly to your destination.

A road service plan is a must for most drivers, and can be well worth its typical $30 to $50 annual fee. Check it out.

# Fire
## How to fight

Car fires are devastating; by the time the fire department arrives on the scene, the car usually has been reduced to a burned-out hulk. However, drivers who carry a small fire extinguisher can often put out a fire before it spreads.

A five-pound dry powder extinguisher rated for Class A, B, and C fires (trash, gasoline, and electrical) will do the job, but it makes a mess that's hard to clean up. And if the dry powder is drawn into a running engine, it can cause expensive damage.

A Halon gas extinguisher, the kind used in race cars, does a better job and causes no damage or mess. Halon extinguishers may be hard to find, but are worth the search. Try hot rod or speed shops, or check your Yellow Pages under "Fire Extinguishers."

Electrical fires caused by short circuits can occur anywhere in the car. Gasoline fires usually start in the engine compartment when leaking gas hits a hot engine part. Keep heavy leather work gloves with your fire extinguisher so you can open the hood without burning your hands. A fire near the gas tank can cause an explosion. Don't even try to put it out; get everyone out of the car and retreat a few hundred feet. Warn off traffic and call for help.

If you smell gas, have a mechanic check the car immediately; it could be a fuel leak, or just a saturated charcoal canister (part of the pollution control system) that needs to be replaced. When you work on the fuel system, be sure the engine is cold, and have rags on hand to mop up spilled gas. Do not restart the engine until all spilled gasoline has evaporated and all odor is gone.

# Fog
## How to get through it

Fog is one of the great equalizers. Even race-car drivers can go no faster than they can see in the fog.

You should do your best to see and be seen in fog. Keep the windshield clean by using the wipers and washers frequently; mist builds up on the glass almost unnoticed and cuts vision drastically.

Drive with the brightest lights you can, so long as they don't bounce back off the fog and cut your vision, or blind oncoming drivers. Use your low beams during the day. On an empty road at night, experiment with your high beams, low beams, and parking lights. In heavy fog you can see further with low beams than high. In a real pea soup fog, even low beams can cause too much glare at night.

This is when fog lights come in handy. Yellow lights work no better than white in most fog (fog lights come in both colors). Their low, wide light pattern with a sharp beam cut-off reduces bounce-back glare and lets you pick out the edge of the road. You can get an extra-bright red rear fog light, too, so that other cars can see you at a greater distance.

On many new cars, the fog lights are wired to work only with the low beams. If it doesn't violate state law, it is worth having them rewired to work independently; that way you can use them with the headlights off (in really thick fog), or with the high beams, where they act as "cornering lights" on twisty roads on fair nights.

Try to relax and use all your senses in the fog. Turn off the radio and open a side window, even if it's cold. Sound travels great distances in fog, and you can often hear an approaching car before you can see it, especially during the day, when the other car may not have its lights on.

Use the right edge of the road as a guide in thick fog. Drive slowly enough so you can stop in the distance that is visible ahead. If you have to creep along, turn on your hazard flashers. If conditions get too bad, pull well off the road before stopping. Never stop on the road—another car is likely to plow into you.

## Four-Wheel-Drive
### All pulling together

Once the province of pickup trucks and Jeeps, four-wheel-drive (4wd) has become a popular option on cars ranging from sports models to family sedans. Trucks use 4wd to drive off-road. On cars, 4wd provides extra traction, as well as a greater safety margin than 2wd, on slick roads.

Many 4wd systems are "part-time"; you have to switch in or out of 4wd as road conditions change, usually by pushing a button or flipping a switch on the dash. There are a few "full-time" systems that are always in 4wd.

The advantages of 4wd are greater safety and less chance of getting stuck in snow, ice, sand, or on wet and slippery roads. Disadvantages include extra cost and complexity, some extra maintenance, and a drop in fuel economy when 4wd is engaged.

## Four-Wheel-Steering
Latest gimmick from the orient

That's not a misprint; several Japanese autos now offer optional four-wheel-steering (4ws) systems, with other car makers expected to follow. The different car makers' systems vary in mechanical execution, but are similar in concept: At low speeds, the rear wheels steer in the opposite direction from the front wheels (though at a much smaller angle). This reduces the car's turning radius, making it much more agile in parking maneuvers and other tight situations.

At highway speeds, the rear wheels turn in the same direction as the fronts. Although the rear wheels move through a very tiny angle (usually less than two degrees), the car is much more stable in fast curves or during lane-change maneuvers.

It is estimated that 4ws increases the car's stability, and therefore your safety margin, by about 10%. However, the effect is so subtle that many drivers may not notice any difference in ordinary driving.

# Frozen Door Locks
## Put the heat on them

Moisture in the air or water from a car wash can freeze inside a door lock in winter, making it impossible to turn the key. Special aerosols containing alcohol and a lubricant are made to thaw frozen car locks. Don't keep the aerosol inside the car! It's small enough to carry in a purse, tote bag, or jacket pocket.

You can work a key into a frozen lock by heating the blade of the key with a cigarette lighter or match before you insert it. If the key does not have a rubber top, wear gloves or hold it with pliers to avoid burning your fingers.

To keep water out, cover door and trunk locks with masking tape before you go through a car wash in winter.

# Fuel Economy
## Getting even with OPEC

The traditional route to maximum fuel economy is well-known: avoid high speeds and jackrabbit starts, keep your engine in tune, and use radial tires. Here are some additional gas-saving tips that few drivers observe:

Keep tires inflated to at least the pressures recommended on the label pasted to the driver's door. If you add up to five psi more, fuel economy and handling will improve. Just don't exceed the maximum pressure molded into the tire sidewall (see TIRE PRESSURE).

Have wheel alignment checked periodically.

Use lightweight 5W-30 oil instead of the more popular 10W-30 or 10W-40. Many car makers now recommend 5W-30 oil. Check your Owner's Manual and follow its advice on oil.

Use cruise control (or self control) to maintain a steady pace on the highway. Speed changes waste gas.

Don't lug around a lot of unnecessary weight in the trunk—extra weight burns more gas.

For the same reason, clear snow off the whole car before driving, not just from the windows.

Keep windows closed on the highway and use the dash vents for fresh air—the vents are quieter and cause less aerodynamic drag, which burns up fuel.

The drag of a roof rack can add 5% to 25% to your fuel bill. Remove a rack, if possible, when it's not needed. When you pack a roof rack, arrange luggage in a wedge shape, tapered toward the front. Cover luggage with a tight-fitting tarp, secured by elastic straps or rope.

# Fuel Filters
## Unclogging a bottle neck

The fuel filter traps rust, sediment, and other gunk from your fuel tank before it can clog up delicate parts of the carburetor or fuel injection system. When the fuel filter gets clogged, it can cause hard starting, rough running, stalling, or backfiring. This is why you should replace the filter once a year, or if it gets clogged from a bad batch of gas.

There are several types of filter. About the only one you would want to change yourself is the cylindrical in-line filter, which is spliced into a fuel line near the carburetor. Make sure the engine is cold, then place a rag under the filter to catch any spilled gas. Loosen the hose clamps and pull the filter from the rubber hoses. Insert the new filter and re-tighten the clamps. Run the engine to check for leaks.

Other filters, located under the car or inside the carburetor, fuel pump, or fuel tank, are more complicated to replace. Leave them to a pro.

# Fuses
## Checking and replacing

Your car's electrical system is protected by fuses, just as fuses protect your house. The fuse box may be under the dash or the hood (see your Owner's Manual). Most new cars use plug-in plastic fuses with two metal tangs. Many older cars have cylindrical glass fuses. A short circuit or overload will burn up the filament inside either kind.

When an electrical accessory goes on the blink, check the fuse box. The fuse box may be labelled to tell you which components each fuse protects. If not, check the Owner's Manual.

You will have to remove a plug-in fuse to see its filament. To remove and replace glass fuses, you need a plastic fuse puller.

Always use a fuse with the correct amperage (the blown one could have been wrong). The correct amperage is usually printed next to the fuse slot on the fuse box. If not, look it up in your Owner's Manual.

If the fuse blows repeatedly, there is a short in the electrical system. See a mechanic.

## Gasoline
### Choosing the one that's right for your car

Despite all the hoopla in oil company advertising, there is not a lot of difference between various gasoline brands. The cheapest one that keeps your car running well is the one for you, with one major caution: some fuel injection systems are easily clogged by deposits that form on the injector nozzles when a hot engine is shut off.

If your car has fuel injection, use a brand of gas with a high detergent level. But shop around—some brands put extra detergent only in their expensive "premium" blends; others put it in all their gasolines. A fuel-injected car that runs rough may have a clogged injector. A few tankfuls of high-detergent gas may be all you need to fix it.

A gasoline's *octane* number is a measure of its resistance to knocking—the pinging or rattling noise you sometimes hear when an engine is straining up a long hill (see PINGING). Continued knocking can cause severe engine damage. If your engine knocks, try switching to a higher octane gas. By law, the octane number of for each type of gasoline must be posted on the pump. If the car continues to knock, see a mechanic.

The octane recommended for your car is given in the Owner's Manual. You may get away with a lower number at high altitudes. If you tow a trailer or put other heavy loads on the engine, you may need a higher octane to prevent knocking.

Some gasoline is blended with *alcohol* to raise its octane and to stretch fuel supplies. Many cars run well on mixtures of up to ten percent ethanol alcohol or five percent methanol alcohol, if blended properly. Methanol may damage the fuel system on some older cars. Check with your dealer.

## Self-serving etiquette

Self-service gas stations are legal in most states, and popular because pumping your own can save several cents per gallon. Doing it yourself is easy if you follow the rules. Always turn off the engine when you pull up to the pump. Give the attendant your credit card or enough cash to cover the gas you need before you do anything else. Then open the gas cap and put it in a clean, safe place, like the top of the gas pump. Do not put it on your car; it will drip gasoline on the paint.

Lift the gas hose nozzle from its cradle on the pump

and lift up the lever under the nozzle—this will turn the pump on and reset its numbers to zero. Place the nozzle into your car's filler neck and squeeze the trigger to start gasoline flowing. Wear gloves in cold weather; gas is stored underground and will make the nozzle ice cold. When the tank is full and gas backs up the filler neck, the nozzle will shut off automatically. Don't squeeze in a few last drops to round off the price; when the cold gasoline warms up and expands in your tank, it may overflow.

When you have finished, push the lever down on the pump and hang up the nozzle. Screw your gas cap back onto the filler neck. Then, get your change from the attendant or sign the credit card receipt.

Remember that you have to check your own tire pressures, oil, and fluid levels when you use self-service stations. This can be done at the station or in your driveway, but you must do it. If you buy self-service gas most of the time, no attendant will do it for you.

## Government Agencies
Getting their undivided attention

Trying to work with the government agencies listed under CONSUMER GROUPS and in other parts of this book can be frustrating. Requests for help or even information sometimes go unanswered. If your request seems like too much work, a civil servant may tell you the information you want is not available or "isn't public."

Aside from military secrets, most government information is available to the general public. If you think you're getting a runaround, send a letter to the head of the agency, with copies to your representatives in the Senate and Congress (this drives bureaucrats nuts and often insures action). Mark both the letter and its envelope "Freedom of Information Act Request."

Briefly restate your request in the letter. By federal law, the government agency has ten working days to respond. You will usually get what you want if you have gone to the right agency in the first place. See CONSUMER GROUPS for a list of who does what.

# Headlights
## How to aim them

If oncoming cars flash their brights at you when you've got your headlights on low beam, the lights probably are aimed too high. If you can hardly see the road ahead at night, your lights are aimed too low. Garages have precision headlight aiming machines. In an emergency, you can do a passably accurate job yourself:

Park the car on a level surface so the bumper touches a wall. Use chalk to make a cross on the wall, centered in front of each light. Back the car 20 to 25 feet away from the wall and turn on the low beams. The bright center of each beam should be below the horizontal line of each cross. If it's not, use a screwdriver to turn the adjusting screws next to each light until the bright spot is centered just below the line. There is an adjusting screw on the top and side of each headlight. On some cars you may have to remove a trim ring to reach these screws. If your car has just two headlights, the job is done.

On cars with four headlights, you must adjust the high-beam lights separately. Cover the outer (high-low beam) lights with cardboard. Switch on the high beams. Adjust the inner (high beam only) lights so their bright spots are centered on the crosses. Replace the trim rings. Have a garage check your aim as soon as possible.

## Replacing a burned out lamp

The headlights on modern cars may be round, rectangular, or flush-fitting aerodynamic units. Flush-fitting lights usually have replaceable bulbs. To reach them, you must open the hood and unscrew the bulb socket from the back of the headlight. Unplug the old bulb and plug in its replacement. Never touch the glass part of a new bulb; the oil on your skin may cause it to burn out prematurely. Hold the bulb with a piece of cloth or a paper towel. Screw the socket with the new bulb into the back of the headlight.

Round and rectangular sealed beam headlamps are replaced as a unit that includes bulb, lens, and reflector. To remove the old headlamp, first remove any trim ring from around the lamp. Loosen the three screws on the retaining ring of a round light, and rotate the ring counterclockwise to remove the ring and headlamp. You must remove the three or four screws on a rectangular retaining ring.

Do not confuse the two aiming screws (which are under the ring) with the retaining screws. Unplug the wiring connector from the back of the headlamp and plug in the new lamp.

Place the retaining ring over the new headlamp so that the slots in the ring fit over the bumps molded into the headlamp. Align the tabs on a round retaining ring with its screws, and turn the ring clockwise to seat it. Tighten the retaining screws. If you haven't disturbed the aiming screws, there is no need to re-aim the headlights.

# Hood Release
## Freeing up a stuck one

An in-car hood release uses a cable to pop open the hood. Moisture and road salt can corrode the mechanism until it's impossible to open the hood. To prevent this, lubricate the moving parts twice a year with white grease or silicone spray. With the hood open, have a helper operate the release so you can see which parts move and need lubrication. If the release freezes, you may have to remove the grille and use pliers or a screwdriver to open the latch.

Sometimes the cable will break at the release under the hood or at the lever inside the car. If you can get hold of the broken end with locking pliers, you may still be able to open the hood. If not, bring the car to a mechanic or body shop.

## Horn Stuck
### How to turn it off

A blaring horn that won't stop is not only embarrassing, but if the engine isn't running, it also can drain the battery until it's dead. The quickest way to silence it is to shut off the engine, open the hood, and locate the horn—it may be hard to see, but it should be easy to find while it's blaring. The wire that supplies electricity to the horn is attached with a pull-off connector. Simply unplug the connector to silence the horn.

If the connector has an exposed metal end, cover it with tape so it cannot short out on other metal parts and blow a fuse. Take the car to a dealer or mechanic as soon as possible to have the horn fixed; it will not work with the wire disconnected. Drive carefully and with the window open, so you can yell at pedestrians and other drivers if necessary, since you won't have a horn to honk.

# Hoses
Diagnosis & correction of hardened arteries

A burst cooling system hose will cause the engine to overheat and leave you stranded. Check the hoses periodically and replace them every four years to prevent a breakdown. Modern cars have four or more coolant hoses—two each to the radiator and heater, and sometimes smaller ones to heat the choke or intake manifold. Be sure to check them all. If any hose is cracked, spongy, brittle, or oil-soaked, replace it immediately.

To replace a hose, drain the radiator (see ANTI-FREEZE). Loosen the clamp at each end of the hose and slide it inward. Gently twist and pull the hose off the metal neck to which it's attached. If the hose is stuck to the neck, slit it with a utility knife and peel it off.

Get a replacement hose designed for your car's make, model, year, and engine. Clean the metal necks with a wire brush. Lubricate the ends of the new hose with antifreeze, then slip two new clamps onto the hose. Push each end of the hose all the way onto its metal neck. Slide a clamp to within a quarter inch of each hose end and tighten it snugly. Refill the cooling system (see ANTIFREEZE) and run the engine to check for leaks.

# Inspections
## How to pass them

State auto inspections vary from the casual once-over by the corner gas station required in New York, to the trial by fire sometimes administered by civil servants at official state inspection stations in New Jersey. Most check safety-related items such as lights, steering, and brakes, plus the performance of the car's pollution control equipment.

The best way to pass inspection, of course, is to always keep your car in good repair and to have the engine tuned up once a year by a competent mechanic. It makes sense to schedule your annual tuneup just before the required inspection. Ask the mechanic to guarantee a tuneup that will pass the upcoming pollution inspection. If it doesn't, go back to the mechanic and have the engine readjusted

Federal law requires all car makers to warrant the performance of the engine's pollution control equipment for five years or 50,000 miles, provided you follow the manufacturer's maintenance schedule and operating requirements (such as using lead-free gas). Since federal anti-pollution requirements are stricter than those in most states, a properly working engine should breeze through the state inspection. If it can't be adjusted to do so, tell the dealer to repair it and file a claim under the Emission System Warranty (see WARRANTIES) if the car has less than 50,000 miles on it and is under five years old.

Tip to men: If your wife or girlfriend is a real fox and has a sense of humor about such things, have her take the car to the state inspection station in a sexy outfit like short shorts and a T-shirt. This often distracts bored civil servants to the point where they'll pass almost any old crock. This has worked many times. The danger is that the inspectors might go over the car with a fine-tooth comb just to keep her around as long as possible.

# Insurance, Buying
## How to shop for the best protection

Several kinds of coverage are included in every auto insurance policy: liability, comprehensive, collision, medical payment, no-fault, and/or uninsured driver. Your state may require minimum amounts in one or more categories for every car you own.

*Liability* insurance pays for the other driver's medical and repair costs—up to the limit of the policy—if the accident was your fault. Except in clear-cut cases, you may have to go to court to determine fault. If the accident was the other driver's fault, his insurance company must pay.

Liability coverage also pays for "pain and suffering" suits, up to the limits of the policy. Your coverage should be high enough to protect your home and business if there is a high judgement against you. Coverage for $1 million or more guarantees that the insurance company's lawyers will do their best to defend you—the first million's on them!

*Comprehensive* insurance pays for damage done to your car by fire, theft, flood, or other disaster. It may also pay for property inside your car that is damaged or stolen.

*Collision* insurance pays for damage done to your car even if the accident is your fault, or the fault of a hit-

and-run or uninsured driver.

Both comprehensive and collision insurance often have a deductible clause. The amount of the deductible (usually $100 to $500) is paid by you before the insurance company pays the balance. The higher the deductible, the lower the cost of the insurance. Neither collision nor comprehensive insurance will pay more than the car's current resale value. It is not usually worth paying the premium for either type of insurance on an older car that's not worth much.

*Medical payment* insurance pays the medical bills for you, your passengers, or anyone hit by your car, no matter who is at fault. This is good insurance to have if you car-pool or carry passengers often. It may duplicate coverage you already have in a personal health policy. If so, consider a higher deductible.

*No-fault* insurance is required in many states. It replaces medical insurance, up to a certain limit. In some no-fault states, a person involved in an accident loses the right to sue for "pain and suffering" unless medical bills are more than a stated amount.

*Uninsured motorist* coverage pays medical costs for a driver and passengers, up to certain limits, if the accident is caused by a hit-and-run driver or one with no insurance. It may duplicate parts of no-fault and medical policies; you should adjust the deductible accordingly.

Shop for insurance carefully. Rates for the same coverage can vary dramatically from one company to another. Rates also vary depending on the age, sex, marital status and driving record of the drivers who use your car, the area the car is driven in, and the car itself. Luxury and sports models cost the most to insure, medium-sized sedans the least. Unmarried males under 25 have the worst accident records and, therefore, the highest insurance rates.

Most companies offer discounts for insuring more than one car, for taking approved driver ed courses, and for low-mileage drivers. The premium for young drivers may be reduced if you can prove that access to the car is limited—for instance, if the driver is away at school without the car for months at a time.

## Insurance Claims
### When to file

Filing an insurance claim may invite a rate increase, depending upon your company's practices. If your car suffers $300 worth of damage and you have a $200 deductible policy, you will receive only $100. But your rates might go up $30 or more for the next three years. Before you file a claim for a relatively small amount, ask your insurance agent to do a cost analysis.

Even if you decide not to file an insurance claim, you should file an accident report with your insurance company and the police (see ACCIDENT REPORTS). This will cover you if the other party later decides to sue you. If you fail to notify your insurance company within a few days, you may not be covered. The report you send to the insurance company should match the one filed with the police. Keep copies of both reports for your records.

## Ignition System
### Checking it out

A gasoline engine needs three things to work: fuel, air, and a spark at the spark plugs. If your car stalls, runs rough, or won't start, there is a problem with the fuel, air, or electrical ignition system. If there is fuel in the gas tank, if air is not restricted by a stuck choke or clogged air filter (see AIR FILTER), and the battery is OK (see BATTERY), then check the ignition system.

Turn off the engine, open the hood, and locate the distributor—a round, black plastic unit with a heavy cable that runs to each spark plug. Some cars have a long black box instead of a distributor, but it still has a cable to each plug. Check both ends of each cable to be sure it is not disconnected. Push each end firmly home.

Smaller wires run from the distributor to various black boxes. These wires have many plastic connectors—make sure the connectors are not open or loose. If you find an open connector with no obvious mate, don't worry about it; it's either for optional equipment that's not on your car, or a test probe for the mechanic's diagnostic equipment.

## Jacking It Up
Raising your car safely

The bumper jack or side-lift jack supplied with most cars is a flimsy device that should be used only for changing tires in an emergency (see TIRE CHANGING). To work under the car, you need drive-up ramps or a hydraulic jack and jack stands.

For complete information on tire changing, first read the jacking instructions found in your Owner's Manual or on labels affixed to the jack or under the trunk lid of your car. Always park the car on firm, level ground. Set the parking brake, and put an automatic transmission into PARK, a manual transmission into REVERSE. Wedge a rock or a piece of lumber up against the tire diagonally opposite the one you want to change, so that the car cannot roll off the jack. For example, if you need to change the right rear tire, chock the left front tire. Keep hands and feet out from under the car at all times in case the jack slips.

A jack comes in several parts that have to be assembled each time it is used. Put the base of a bumper jack on the ground and fit the long, toothed stand into it. Slide the lifting device over the stand and insert the handle (usually the lug wrench) into the pivoting tube on the lift. On side-lift scissors jacks, fit the crank into the bracket at one end of the jack.

Position the jack near the tire to be changed. A bumper jack fits into one of four slots in the bumper. A side-lift jack mates with fittings under the side of the car, between the wheels. If the car is off the pavement, place a wide board (or heavy cardboard) under the jack so it won't sink into the ground. Pump the handle on a bumper jack to raise the car. Turn the crank on a scissors jack.

To lower the car, flip the direction lever on the lift of a bumper jack and pump the handle. To lower a scissors jack, turn the crank in the opposite direction. Remove the wheel chock before you drive away.

## Jump Starting
How to boost a dead battery

You can start a car with a discharged battery if you have a set of jumper cables and access to a running car. But be careful not to cause a spark, which can ignite the explosive hydrogen gas given off by a battery being charged. It's a good idea to wear safety glasses and gloves when working under the hood to jump-start a car.

Bring both cars nose to nose, without touching bumpers, then shut off their engines and open their hoods. Set both parking brakes, and put automatic transmissions into PARK, manuals into NEUTRAL.

Identify the positive and negative posts on each battery (usually marked POS, +, NEG, or -). Attach the jumper cable with the red clamps to the positive posts on each battery. Attach the cable with black clamps to the negative post of the good battery, and to a good ground on the engine of the car with the dead battery, such as the alternator bracket. Do not attach this clamp to the negative post of the dead battery (as is so commonly done). The negative cable can spark and should be kept far from the dead battery.

Keep hands and cables clear of all fans, pulleys, and belts. Start the engine of the car with the good battery. Then start the engine with the dead battery. If it still won't start, you need a mechanic.

Remove the black cable from both cars, starting with the booster car; then remove the red cable. Drive the car with the discharged battery for at least 20 minutes so the alternator can recharge the battery.

# L

## Lawyers
### Finding the right one

Lawyers are a bit like doctors...you wouldn't go to an ear specialist for an eyeglass prescription. Lawyers specialize too, and you need to find the right one for auto-related problems. Your family lawyer may be real nice, and perfect for wills or a house closing, but you need a specialist if you are involved in an accident suit, criminal charges, or an unjustified arrest for drunk driving.

Now that attorneys are allowed to advertise, you can find them listed in the Yellow Pages, but you'll want a better recommendation than that.

The Center for Auto Safety (2001 S St. NW, Washington, DC 20009) can recommend lawyers with experience in auto repair and warranty complaints. Your local bar association should be able to recommend lawyers who specialize in the area you need. Just tell them what kind of case you have, and that you want an experienced specialist, not a "general practitioner." Also ask friends, co-workers, and your union or employer if they can recommend a specialist they have had good experience with. You can check the background of recommended lawyers in the *Martindale-Hubbell Law Directory*, available in law libraries and metropolitan public libraries.

Call the lawyers who seem qualified to handle your case and arrange for an initial consultation. Ask what the fee will be for this meeting. Determine on the phone whether the lawyer has experience in the area you need, and his or her fees. Bring any and all documentation to this first meeting. The lawyer will need to know the facts of your case. But make sure there's time to discuss payment and experience fully. Ask for a win-loss record in your type of case. The lawyer may be vague (it's a poor record), or claim 90% success, in which case you should ask for documentation in the most diplomatic way possible. Some attorneys may resent such quizzing, but how else can you determine whether you've got the right one?

At the end of this interview, you both should have enough information to make a "yes" or "no" decision about each other.

## Leaks, Fluid
### What is that puddle under the car?

Fluid leaking from your car can be perfectly normal, or a sign of trouble. A puddle of clear water under the middle of the car in the summer is probably condensation from the air conditioner, and nothing to worry about.

Green or yellowish water with a faint sweet smell found near the engine is antifreeze; check the cooling system for leaks.

Dark red fluid with a distinctive odor is probably from the automatic transmission. You can check it against the fluid on the transmission dipstick. Have a mechanic inspect the transmission. Power steering fluid is similar. Check the fluid level in the power steering reservoir.

An oily liquid with little color may be brake fluid. Look for a low level in the brake fluid reservoir.

A brown or black slippery fluid is motor oil. Check the drain plug and other points under the engine for leaks.

Thin fluid with a strong smell is gasoline. Check fuel lines and carburetor for leaks. If the leak is large, don't start the engine; call for a tow truck or the fire department.

Puddles in your driveway or garage are most likely from your car. Those you discover in a parking lot may be from previous cars. When you get home, spread newspaper under the car and check later to see if the leak persists.

## Leaks, Wind and Water
Keeping Mother Nature in her place

Gaps in the weatherstripping around the windows, doors, and trunk can cause wind whistles as you drive and allow dust or rainwater to leak in. Tracking down a leak can be tricky, since water can travel some distance from the leak before it drips or accumulates in a puddle.

The only way to find a suspected leak around the windshield or fixed rear window is to run a gentle stream of water around the outside of the glass while a helper inside the car checks for leaks. Once you pinpoint the entry point, mark it with masking tape and allow the glass and gaskets to dry thoroughly. Pry the gasket away from the glass just enough to spread a bead of silicone sealer under the gasket in the leaking area.

If the weatherstripping around doors, moving windows, or the trunk is damaged, replace it with new weatherstripping, bought from your car dealer. Loose weatherstripping that is sound can be reglued with special weatherstrip adhesive, sold in auto parts stores.

Weatherstripping that looks OK may have low spots that allow leaks. To check the seal, rub soft artist's chalk along the entire weatherstrip, then close the door or trunk. Open it again and check the line of chalk that's been transferred to the weatherstripping's contact area. Low spots will show up as gaps in the chalk line. To elevate low spots, unglue the weatherstripping with release agent, sold in professional auto parts stores. Shim up the low spots with pieces of thin cardboard or slivers of household weatherstripping, then reglue it in place.

## Leasing versus Buying
### Which is the best deal?

At first blush, leasing a car rather than buying it seems to have many advantages. Under the new income tax laws, you can no longer deduct sales tax, and the amount of interest that you can deduct from an auto loan is dwindling fast.

On the plus side, there is little or no down payment on a lease. Monthly payments are lower than buying, so you can often afford a bigger, flashier car. There is no loan interest to pay. You pay only to use the car, not to own a depreciating asset. You don't have to worry about trade-in value or selling the car privately when you're ready for a new one. If you lease a car that suffers an unexpected loss of resale value (as GM diesels and Audi 5000s have), it is the lessor's problem, not yours. If you are strapped for monthly payments and not overly concerned with the total cost, leasing can make sense.

But, overall, leasing is more costly than buying. At the end of a typical four- or five-year lease, you have nothing to show for your payments; at the end of a similar period of ownership, you still have a car worth several thousand dollars. If you pay cash for a car rather than financing it, your savings when buying, vs. leasing, are even greater.

At the end of the lease period, you may also have to pay a penalty charge for excess mileage or damage that would lower the car's resale value to the lessor. If you decide you don't like the car and want to terminate the lease early, there is a penalty for that, too. If the leased car is stolen or destroyed, the insurance may pay only for the car's depreciated value. The lessor is still entitled to the balance of the lease payments plus the resale value in the contract. You may have to make up for any shortfall.

# Lemon Laws
How to use them

The proverbial "lemon"—the car that can't be fixed—used to be the buyer's problem. Today, the vast majority of states and the District of Columbia have Lemon Laws that can force a manufacturer to buy back a troublesome car. Such laws put the heat on car makers and their dealers to be more conscientious and less cavalier about warranty repairs.

Lemon laws are slightly different in each state, but as a rule they define a lemon as a car that has been back to the dealer three or four times without success to repair the same problem, or has been off the road for a total of 15 to 30 business days during the first year of ownership.

The whole point of a Lemon Law is to set up a formal procedure that avoids the hassle and expense of suing a car maker over a lemon. The drill in most states is this: if your car meets the legal lemon definition, you must notify the manufacturer (or, in some states, the dealer) in writing that you are filing a Lemon Law complaint. Send copies to your state senator and assemblyman; this often gets action (especially in an election year), and puts a little more heat on the dealer, who is likely to be a campaign contributor.

After you give notice of a Lemon Law action, the manufacturer usually gets one more try to fix the car. If that fails, you will be asked to take your case to arbitration.

Local arbitration boards will hear your case (no lawyers are required or permitted) and the dealer's story, then give a decision. The board's decision is binding on the dealer, but may not be on the consumer. If you don't like the decision, you can still sue. If the dealer doesn't like it, that's tough (see ARBITRATION for details).

If the manufacturer has to buy back or replace your car, you won't get back your original purchase price. The manufacturer is allowed to deduct a reasonable amount for the mileage you have already put on the car.

For specific details on the Lemon Law in your state, write to the Attorney General's office in your state capital.

# Light Trucks
## One out of three new "cars" *isn't*

For every two cars sold in America, one light truck is purchased. Some of these vans, pickups, and utility vehicles are used commercially, but the vast majority are used as substitutes for, or supplements to, the family car. These trucks come in many shapes and sizes. The traditional "full-size" truck is pretty big, and, though useful, can be unwieldy and difficult to drive. Newer "compact" or "mini" sizes are more car-like in their handling, and are responsible for the popularity of light trucks.

Vans range in size from small minis, which threaten to replace the traditional family station wagon, to the big 15-seaters favored by airport "limo" services. Many dealers offer customized vans with picture windows, plush sofa-like seats, and other comforts. These can be fun if the quality of the add-on equipment is up to factory standards. If it's not, you may find yourself stuck with an expensive white elephant.

Pickup trucks are seen as the original American sports cars by many enthusiasts. Some can be ordered from the factory with a wide variety of special equipment, including dual rear wheels for heavy payloads, four-door/six-seat crew cabs, two-door/four-seat extended cabs, or traditional cabs with a single bench seat. Most can be ordered with all the comfort and convenience options of a fancy sedan. In some cases, it is possible to put more than $7000 worth of options onto a pickup that starts out with an attractively low base price. Caps (bolt-on roofs for the open cargo bed) are a particularly popular pickup option.

Utility vehicles like the Jeep Cherokee, Ford Bronco, and Chevy Blazer are enormously popular. Shorter but taller than the average station wagon, some of them have as much cargo room inside, and most offer the option of four-wheel drive for surer footing in ice and snow, or the ability to drive in rough terrain if you must.

# Loans
## Getting the best deal on wheels

The super-low interest loans, offered by some car makers as incentives to buy whenever business is bad, have changed the entire ballgame when it comes to buying a car. Paying cash always used to be cheaper in the long run than financing a car. But when manufacturers offer loans at well below the market rate, it may cost you less to keep your money in the bank, say at 6% interest, if the car maker is offering loans at 3%.

When comparing car loans from different places, there are three important things to consider: the annual percentage rate (APR); the total interest payment (or finance charge); and the monthly payment. Compare all three before making a final choice.

Car loans are available from banks, car dealers, auto manufacturers, credit unions, insurance companies, and finance companies. Shop around as carefully for the loan as you did for the car. You may find that the fabulous car maker's loan at 3.9% or 2.9% or even 0% is only for a 12-month loan that carries monthly payments so high they will ruin your budget. A three-, four-, or five-year loan may have a much higher APR, combining attractively low monthly payments with a total finance charge that runs into thousands of dollars.

If the dealer has to help pay the cost of a very low interest rate, he may charge you more for the car than he would to a buyer who doesn't want the rock bottom rate. Look in the advertising or loan agreement for the telltale phrase, "Dealer contribution may affect purchase price."

See the chart below for a comparison of the monthly payments and total cost of loans at different APRs.

As a general rule, used car loans carry higher APRs and run for shorter periods than new car loans.

Finance companies usually charge the highest rates because they lend money to the poorest risks. A passbook loan from your bank can have a very low rate, which is the difference between the APR of the loan and the interest your savings are earning. But you must keep at least the outstanding amount of the loan in your account. You can sometimes borrow against a whole life insurance policy at a low rate, too. But any unpaid loan balance will be subtracted from the death benefit if you die.

Before you sign any loan agreement, read all the fine print and be sure you understand it fully. Do not sign an agreement that has an incorrect statement or figure, just because you have been given verbal assurance that it means something else. Some dealers have been known to trick buyers into signing 21% loans with the assurance that the figure was a "typo" and really was 12%!

## INTEREST CHARGES ON EACH $1000 BORROWED

| APR | 1 Year | | 2 Years | | 3 Years | | 4 Years | |
|---|---|---|---|---|---|---|---|---|
| | MONTHLY PAYMENT | TOTAL FINANCE CHARGE | MONTHLY PAYMENT | TOTAL FINANCE CHARGE | MONTHLY PAYMENT | TOTAL FINANCE CHARGE | MONTHLY PAYMENT | TOTAL FINANCE CHARGE |
| 0% | $83 | 0 | $42 | 0 | $28 | 0 | $21 | 0 |
| 2.9% | $85 | $ 16 | $43 | $ 30 | $29 | $ 45 | $22 | $ 60 |
| 3.9% | $85 | $ 21 | $43 | $ 41 | $29 | $ 61 | $23 | $ 81 |
| 4.9% | $86 | $ 27 | $44 | $ 52 | $30 | $ 77 | $23 | $103 |
| 5.9% | $86 | $ 32 | $44 | $ 62 | $30 | $ 93 | $23 | $125 |
| 7.9% | $87 | $ 43 | $45 | $ 84 | $31 | $126 | $24 | $169 |
| 10% | $88 | $ 55 | $46 | $108 | $32 | $162 | $25 | $218 |
| 12% | $89 | $ 66 | $47 | $130 | $33 | $196 | $26 | $264 |
| 14% | $90 | $ 77 | $48 | $152 | $34 | $230 | $27 | $312 |
| 18% | $92 | $100 | $50 | $198 | $36 | $302 | $29 | $410 |

*Figures rounded off to the nearest dollar
Sources: Ford Finance; General Motors Acceptance Corp.

## Interest charges on each $1000 borrowed

Find the annual percentage rate (APR) at the left that applies to your loan, then move right to the columns under the length of your loan. To figure your monthly payment and total finance charge, multiply the numbers by the amount (in thousands) of your loan. For example, multiply by 10 for a $10,000 loan, by 8.5 for an $8,500 loan, or by 7.35 for a $7,350 loan.

# Locked Out, Keys Lost
## How to break into your own car

It's a good idea to always carry an extra car key on your person—in a pocket with your loose change, for instance, or on a key ring attached to your belt. Never carry it in your wallet or purse; if it is lost or stolen, a thief will have your license, registration, home address, and car key—almost an engraved invitation to drop by at night and drive off with your car. For the same reason, avoid key holders with your name and address, unless it's a post office box number.

If other family members have a key to your car, call them at home or work, if possible, and ask them to bring the key to you. If that's not practical, call the police; they often have car-opening tools for such emergencies. So do some car dealers and gas stations.

If the car has button-type inside door locks, you can often open them with a coat hanger. Straighten out the hanger and form a loop in one end. Force the wire between the window glass and weatherstripping as close to the lock button as possible. Bend the hanger as needed to reach the lock button. Slip the loop around the stem of the lock button and pull it up. This technique works best on mushroom-shaped buttons, but sometimes works on cylindrical ones, too.

If all else fails, call a locksmith who advertises emergency car entries (see the Yellow Pages) and be prepared for a hefty bill!

# M

## Mechanics
### The good, the bad, and/or the ugly

Finding a good mechanic is a bit like finding a good doctor or lawyer. First, you should have some idea whether your car's problem will require a specialist or a general practitioner. Then ask friends and co-workers for recommendations. Check out the shop to see if it looks clean, orderly, well-run, and if it is equipped with the electronic diagnostic equipment needed to cope with today's computer-controlled cars.

Several organizations can help steer you to a competent garage. Your local Better Business Bureau can tell you if any formal complaints have been lodged against a particular shop.

Look for the blue signs and shoulder patches that identify mechanics certified by the National Institute for Automotive Service Excellence (ASE). This group tests mechanics periodically in eight areas of car repair, from bodywork to transmission repair. Naturally, you want a mechanic who is certified in the kind of work you need.

The AAA's Approved Auto Repair program inspects and approves garages in 26 states, and arbitrates disputes for AAA members. You do not have to be a member to take advantage of an approved shop—just look for the red and blue AAA Approved Auto Repair sign. But don't confuse it with the AAA Emergency Repair Service sign, which is the club's towing service and a whole other ball game.

Automatic transmission, air conditioner, window glass, radiator, and body repairs are best done by specialists. Muffler and brake shops are a mixed bag—

some do good work at reasonable prices, others do fast and dirty jobs on cars they don't expect to see again for years. If you have a good relationship with a general repair shop, they will usually send such work out to a specialty shop and charge you a markup. But it's often worth the premium because an experienced garage knows which specialists are trustworthy and which ones are crooked. The specialty shop may also give your garage a discount that's not available to walk-in customers, so the final price may be much the same.

New car dealers should be able to fix most problems on late-model cars, but they charge the highest prices.

Whichever shop you choose, start them on some simple maintenance work and see if you're happy with it before you trust them with a major job. Build up a good relationship and don't sneak off to a chain store for a cheap muffler—your regular mechanic will spot it next time and may hold it against you. Ask for advice first. An honest mechanic may confide: "Sure, they do that job well and we can't match their prices." He should also advise you to get their best-quality muffler.

Most complaints about dishonest mechanics involve breakdowns far from home where you can't deal with your regular garage, or work done at specialty shops (like brake, muffler, or transmission chains) that do not expect to see your repeat business. Here are some common dirty tricks:

Short sticking—inserting the dipstick only part way into the engine to produce a false "low" reading. When too much oil is then added to the engine, it may froth and not lubricate properly, leading to an expensive breakdown.

Cut belts—a grease monkey "inspecting" the engine slices a fan belt in two with a razor blade, then sells you a high-priced replacement. True broken belts have ragged ends—as though they have been torn apart—not clean cuts.

Leaking shocks—the mechanic replacing a muffler squirts some oil onto a shock absorber, then tells you you've "got a leaker" that needs replacement. And you should always replace shocks in pairs (which is true). Real leaking shocks are covered with road grime, not clean oil.

There are scores of others. Your best defense is to keep your car in good repair to reduce the chance of a breakdown. Look for shops with ASE mechanics or AAA approval, even in an emergency. Ask the mechanic for an estimate, and a full explanation of what needs to be done. Then discuss alternatives. Ask if a lower-priced temporary repair would get you home (to your trusted mechanic). Ask to see any parts that are replaced.

Try to watch the mechanic at all times, without constantly pestering him. Those signs that say "Due To Insurance Regulations, No Customers Permitted In Repair Bay" are usually a bluff by mechanics who don't want to be coached. If you promise to behave and enter at your own risk, there should be no objection to keeping an eye on the job. At the very least, you can then be fairly sure that the damaged parts they show you actually came from your car.

If possible, pay by credit card. If there is a problem later, you then have some recourse (see COMPLAINTS).

# N

## Nader, Ralph
Consumer's champion

Much of the auto safety legislation and consumer help programs for car buyers in America can be credited to an activist lawyer named Ralph Nader. His devastating book about the Chevrolet Corvair, called *Unsafe at Any Speed*, although criticized in the automotive press as being inaccurate and uninformed, started the ball rolling for the consumer. GM's ham-handed attempt to sic private detectives on Nader only strengthened his hand and his credibility.

When the National Highway Traffic Safety Administration didn't seem to be doing the job Nader envisioned for government, he started his own watchdog group called the Center for Auto Safety. Although Nader often receives letters from disgruntled consumers, he does not handle individual complaints; direct these to the Center for Auto Safety, 2001 S St. NW, Washington, DC 20009 with a stamped, self-addressed return envelope (see CONSUMER GROUPS).

## Oil Changes
### How often is enough?

Oil never wears out, but the chemical additives that slow corrosion, neutralize acids, and hold dirt in suspension do wear out as the months and miles add up. Most dirt is trapped by the oil filter, but smaller particles circulate through the engine with the oil. When you change the oil and filter (or have them changed), you remove this dirt and replenish the additive supply.

Your Owner's Manual will tell you how often the car maker wants you to change the oil and filter. But be sure to read the fine print. Most manuals list oil change intervals of up to 7,500 miles or 12 months for "normal" driving, which is defined as long trips at highway speeds on paved roads in moderate weather. These are fairly abnormal conditions, compared to the short trips and stop-and-go around-town driving that most people do. For these "severe" conditions, most car makers recommend oil change intervals of 3,000-4,000 miles or three to four months, whichever comes first.

If you drive on unpaved or dusty roads, or have a diesel or turbocharged engine, you should change the oil even more often. Most mechanics suggest changing oil every 3,000 miles or three months. Compared with the price of a rebuilt engine, or a brand new car, the cost of an oil change is insignificant.

## Oil Level
### Checking it; adding more

Every engine is equipped with a dipstick—a primitive

but effective device for checking the amount of oil in the crankcase (the oil reservoir at the bottom of the engine). As its name implies, it's a stick that dips into the oil. The amount of oil clinging to the dipstick tells you how much is in the crankcase. To correctly read the oil level, do the following:

Park on level ground, shut off the engine, and wait a few minutes for all the oil to drain back into the crankcase. Open the hood and find the oil dipstick, which is yellow or labelled OIL on many newer cars. Do not confuse it with the automatic transmission dipstick (oil is amber or black; transmission fluid is red or brown).

Remove the dipstick, wipe it clean with a paper towel, and insert it all the way back into its tube (if you do not push it all the way down, the oil level will read low—a favorite trick of dishonest mechanics). Pull the stick out again and note the level of the oil on the blade. Most dipsticks are marked FULL and ADD. The correct oil level is between those two lines. If the oil is at or below the ADD mark, you should add one quart, let it drain into the crankcase, then recheck the level.

Do not add oil if the level is above the ADD mark; if you overfill the crankcase, the crankshaft may stir up the oil, causing it to foam and lubricate poorly.

Some dipsticks simply have two unlabeled lines or notches. The top one (closest to the handle) is the FULL mark, and the bottom one (closest to the end of the blade) is the ADD mark. A few say MAX and MIN. The minimum mark means the oil is one quart low.

Check your oil level once a week, or every time you get gas. If the oil level is low, it's easy to add a quart now that oil is sold in plastic bottles with screw caps. Be sure to use the correct oil for your car (see OIL TYPES). Make sure the engine is off. Find the oil filler cap at the top of the engine (usually marked OIL) and

O

remove it. Remove the cap from the oil bottle, plus any plastic ring around the neck or foil seal over the spout. Pour the oil into the filler, then screw the filler cap on tightly. Wait a few minutes after adding oil, then check the oil level again.

# Oil Types
## Choosing the right kind

Your Owner's Manual will tell you what type of oil the manufacturer recommends for your car under various driving conditions. Some specify different weights for winter and summer, others specify the same oil all year long. To keep your warranty in effect, you must follow the Owner's Manual scrupulously.

When shopping for oil, you will find it has two classifications: a service classification by the American Petroleum Institute (API), and a weight classification by the Society of Automotive Engineers (SAE). Never consider buying an oil without ratings by both these organizations.

The API service ratings of oil for gasoline engines run from SA (an obsolete type possibly suitable for door hinges) to SF, which is what you want in a modern car. The API's next rating, when it's issued, will be SG. Oil for diesel engines is rated CC or CD.

The SAE weight classifications are also called viscosity grades. They run from 5 (the thinnest oil) to 90 or more (for the heaviest oil, used in rear axles). Thinner oils flow sooner in cold engines, heavier oils hold up better in hot engines. Most motor oils have additives called viscosity improvers, which allow one oil to cover several weight ratings, such as 10W-30. The "W" means that the oil is suitable for low-temperature winter use.

A relatively thin 5W-30 is recommended in many new cars for better fuel economy—thinner oil puts less drag on an engine's internal parts. The most popular oil—10W-40—has so much viscosity improver that it may cause damaging deposits inside the engine, especially in diesels.

Synthetic oils cost quite a bit more than conventional mineral oils, but they offer several advantages: they flow better at sub-zero temperatures, hold up better at very high temperatures, and can go longer between changes.

## Out of Gas
How to handle

Check the gas gauge every time you get into the car. Running out of gas is not only inconvenient, it can stir up rust and sediment from the bottom of the tank and clog fuel filters. If you do run out of gas, turn on the emergency flashers and try to coast well off the road (see BREAKDOWNS). Check the fuel gauge to make sure that fuel is really the problem. If the gauge reads empty, you will have to call for help or go for gas.

If you decide to go for gas, don't hitchhike to a gas station—hitchhiking can be dangerous. If you're in an inhabited area, walk to nearby houses and see if the homeowners can sell you any gas they may have for lawnmowers, and if they will loan you a gas can. Just a gallon or two may be enough to get you to a gas station. A few gallons of leaded gasoline won't do any permanent damage to a car that requires lead-free gas.

## Overheating
### Keeping your cool when your car can't

Your car can overheat due to a mechanical fault, such as a split radiator hose or a broken fan belt, or because the design of the cooling system is simply inadequate to handle the load on a hot day. A water temperature gauge can give you warning of trouble if you notice it creeping up toward the danger zone. A TEMP warning light usually won't go on until it is too late.

A car is more likely to overheat when stuck in heavy traffic than if it is moving briskly. If your car is prone to overheating, try to avoid traffic jams and get onto side roads where traffic is moving freely.

If you are stuck in a traffic jam, shift into NEUTRAL and rev the engine periodically. This will increase coolant flow through the engine and draw more air through the radiator if you have a belt-driven fan (not electric). Turn off the air conditioner, which adds heat to the engine compartment. As a last resort, turn the heater on high—this will draw heat away from the engine.

If the radiator boils over despite your best efforts, pull off the road and call for help (see BREAK-DOWNS). Wait at least 15 minutes for the engine to cool down before attempting to open the hood. If the radiator is blocked by bugs and debris, clean it off with a soft brush or a hose.

Look for coolant leaks, burst hoses, or broken fan belts. If there are no obvious faults, place a heavy towel over the radiator cap and, without pressing down, slowly turn it to the first stop. Be careful—boiling water may shoot out of the overflow tube. When steam stops coming out of the overflow tube, use the towel to press down on the radiator cap and unscrew it.

When the system cools down, slowly add a 50/50 mix of water and antifreeze to the radiator. If no anti-freeze is available, add water; drain the system and add a proper coolant mixture as soon as possible (see ANTIFREEZE).

# Owner's Manual
## Your car's "Bible"

Next to Gideon Bibles found in hotel rooms, the Owner's Manual that comes with every car is among the least-read books in the world. That's a shame, because the typical Owner's Manual not only tells you such obvious things as how to work all the knobs and switches (which is less than obvious on some of today's more complex cars), but also such vital information as what kind of oil to use, how often to change it, how to perform routine preventive maintenance checks, break-in instructions, where to find the fuses and how to change them, etc. If you've lost your Owner's Manual, you can get a new one by writing to the manufacturer (see CAR COMPANIES) or to the Customer Relations Department of the nearest Zone Office (your dealer has that address).

# P

## Paint Touch-up
### A dab in time will save you nine

Nicks, scratches, and blisters in the paint are an invitation to rust, which can spread like a disease and ruin an otherwise good car. (Colorful auto body repairmen refer to rust as "cancer.") Check your car for chips and scratches often—whenever you wash it is a good time. You can repair minor paint damage yourself with touch-up paint, which is sold in aerosol cans or small bottles by auto parts stores or car dealers.

Buy only paint labelled for your car make, model, year, and color. It may not match exactly, because your car's paint has faded and weathered somewhat. You will also need the primer recommended for use with your car's paint, and a rust "converter," which changes the chemical composition of the rust so that it no longer eats into the bodywork.

For small chips and blisters, scrape away loose paint and rust with the corner of a razor blade, then wipe the area with rust converter. Clean the area with a mild detergent, rinse well, and dry thoroughly with a paper towel. Apply primer with an artist's brush. When the primer dries, apply the touch-up paint with a small brush. If the primer or touch-up paint is only available in aerosol cans, spray a little bit into a paper cup and apply with a brush. If you don't have a brush, you can use the torn end of a paper match for small nicks.

For bigger blisters or long scratches, you'll need aerosol paints. Sand away rust with No. 400 wet sandpaper, treat it with converter, clean and dry the area, then spray on the primer and paint.

To spray small areas, cut a one-inch hole in a piece of cardboard, hold it an inch or two from the car, and spray through the hole. This will confine the spray without leaving the ridge of paint left by masking tape.

When the paint has had several days to dry, smooth the painted area with polishing compound (not the more abrasive rubbing compound). Do not wax repaired areas for 90 days.

PARKING
STOP HERE

DOTY

## Parking Lots and Garages
Entrusting your car to the great unwatched

Parking your car in an urban lot or garage often leads to well-justified fears of theft or damage. If you park at the same lot regularly, the best way to assure courteous service is to quickly establish yourself as a generous tipper. Give something to the kid who retrieves your car, and find an excuse at least once a month to slip a few bucks to the lot manager; this will usually work wonders. If you leave at the same time every day, don't be surprised to find your car front and center, while other car owners have to wait.

If you would like such service and haven't been getting it, call the garage just before you leave work and ask them to bring your car up front for you. Be sure to tip the kid who actually brought the car up, not just the cashier or manager who hands over the keys.

When parking in a strange area, try to find a lot where you can park and lock the car yourself. If that's not possible, pick a lot run by a big chain over a no-name independent operation. If you don't like the looks of the place or its staff when you first pull in, just back out and try another. If the attendant roars off in your car like it's the start of the Indy 500, demand the car back immediately, pay the minimum charge, and park elsewhere.

Tell the attendant you expect to be back in less than an hour, even if you know you will be longer. That way, the car will be kept near the front where there is less chance of vandalism or theft of parts (battery swaps are a favorite trick). Lock the trunk and glove compartment, and leave only the ignition key. Do not leave any valuables in the car, including radar detectors, CB sets, or the radio, if it's a removable type (see RADIO THEFT).

Look over all sides of the car when it's returned to you, and immediately report any damage to the manager, who will often have a Polaroid camera on hand for insurance claims. Most big parking chains are pretty blasé about such damage, but don't get into an argument with the garage staff. If there's a dispute that can't be resolved peacefully, call the cops from the nearest pay phone.

# Pinging
## Your engine's death rattle

The metallic rattling noise you sometimes hear when an engine is straining uphill or accelerating on level ground is called pinging, knocking, or pre-ignition. What is happening is an abnormal, explosive combustion of the gasoline inside the engine, rather than the smooth, even burning that the car's engineers intended. Excessive or prolonged pinging can overheat engine parts and lead to serious damage.

Pinging can be caused by incorrect ignition timing, an overheated engine, faulty pollution control equipment, red-hot carbon deposits inside the engine, or the wrong grade of fuel (see GASOLINE). If the car has not overheated and you are unable to cure the problem by switching to a higher-octane gas, see a mechanic. Don't believe the excuse that pinging is "the sound of economy." Some lean-running engines are prone to pinging, but it can usually be corrected.

# Police
## How to handle the fuzz

If you're stopped by the police, let the officer speak first. Answer politely and look him straight in his mirror sunglasses. Keep your answers brief and never volunteer information. Unless you are a proven smooth talker, or a very pretty lady, it's difficult to strike up a breezy conversation with a cop who is holding a summons book.

Police are often jumpy about being shot at from a stopped car. Stay in your seat as the officer approaches, keeping both hands on top of the steering wheel. Don't make any sudden or unexpected moves. If it is dark out, turn on your interior light as soon as you stop. If the trooper asks for your license and registration, state where it is (wallet, glove compartment, etc.), then say "I'm going to get it now, OK?" Such courtesies are usually appreciated by police, and set a useful tone of cooperation.

If the police want to search your car, truck, or motor home, a search warrant is not required *if the officer has probable cause* to believe there is contraband or evidence of a crime in the car. The legal definition of "probable cause" is a moving cloud of smoke best left to lawyers. If you have nothing to hide, it is best to consent to a search. If you demand a warrant and the officer is serious about the search, your car may be impounded until a warrant is obtained. If evidence is obtained against you illegally, a good lawyer can get it thrown out of court (but not out of the local newspaper...).

If the officer accuses you of drunken driving or speeding, see those sections in this book. If you are stopped for an equipment violation, such as a burned-out light or bald tire, claim ignorance of the problem, express your thanks for having it pointed out, and offer to have the condition fixed immediately. If the officer seems bent on issuing a ticket, repeat that you were not aware of the problem and ask if you could be issued a warning instead.

Never get into an argument with a belligerent cop. Note his badge number and complain to his superiors later. If you think your rights have been violated, consult a lawyer. If it happens in your home town, complain to the mayor and police commissioner, especially if it's a small town where they know you.

# Power Steering Fluid
How to check and add to it

The heart of the power steering system is a belt-driven hydraulic pump mounted near the engine. This pump has a reservoir with a screw cap on it. On many cars, there is a dipstick under the cap for reading the level of fluid in the reservoir. On pumps without a dipstick, the fluid should be a half to one inch from the top of the reservoir.

At least twice a year, and before long trips, check the fluid in the reservoir. This is usually done with the engine at normal operating temperature, although some dipsticks have HOT and COLD markings.

Turn off the engine, open the hood, and locate the power steering pump and reservoir. Wipe any dirt off the cap, then unscrew it and check the level of the fluid clinging to the dipstick, being careful not to touch hot engine parts. If the fluid is below the FULL mark, add the type of fluid called for in your Owner's Manual (some cars use automatic transmission fluid, others require special power steering fluid).

# Push Starts
Raising the dead

You can start a car with a manual transmission and a dead battery by pushing it, either by hand or with another vehicle. If you use another vehicle, make sure the bumpers are the same height and will not override one another, causing body damage. If you intend to push the car by hand, you should have several strong helpers and a bit of level or downhill road in front of the stalled car. The best way to start the car rolling is to have your helpers put their backs against the car and push with their weight and legs.

Turn the ignition on, put the transmission in NEU-TRAL, release the parking brake, and have your helpers push the stalled car up to about 10 mph. When you reach that speed, wave off your pushers, shift into SECOND, and engage the clutch. This should turn the engine fast enough to start it, as long as a dead battery was its only problem. The alternator will keep the engine running, but be sure to drive the car or let the engine run for at least 20 minutes to recharge the battery.

Too many unsuccessful push starts may dump raw fuel into the exhaust system, causing the catalytic converter to overheat when the engine finally starts. If your car doesn't start after one or two tries, call for professional help (see EMERGENCY ROAD SERVICE and TOW TRUCKS).

# R

# Radar Detectors
Electronic countermeasures for the road

Radar detectors are legal in most states. They receive police speed radar signals and warn you when you are approaching a radar trap. Depending upon your point of view, this is only fair, or a license to break the law.

Morality aside, police radar has a lot of faults, in both design and use. Interference from CB radios, motion-detecting burglar alarms and door openers, and other microwave signals can give false speed readings.

After recording an illegal speed, a radar operator must then visually determine which car caused it. Because the radar beam is so wide, it could be a car coming toward the radar or going away from it. It could be the first car in a group or the last. Visually identifying the fastest car is radar's Achilles heel. As a general rule, the first car in a group approaching the officer gets the ticket, no matter who was speeding. It's a bum rap like this that makes radar detectors so popular, despite prices of $100 to over $300.

A radar detector lights up like a Christmas tree and sounds an alarm in the presence of X-band or K-band microwave transmissions, the two frequencies assigned to police radar by the FCC. A good detector can pick up police radar from miles away on a flat road. The detector's audible and visual signals increase the closer you get to the radar source. A police officer cannot make a visual identification at much more than a quarter of a mile.

Radar police like to lurk around corners and over the brows of hills, but even here a good detector can pick up the radar signals reflected off trees, shrubbery, bridges, guardrails, and other traffic.

The latest nuance in the Radar Wars is instant-on radar, which emits no signal until the officer fires it at an approaching car. With no advance warning, your detector's alarms are triggered suddenly, and the message is "Gotcha!" But even here you have some defense. Your detector may pick up preliminary beeps as the officer fires the radar gun at cars ahead of yours.

Even if your detector suddenly bursts into full shriek when it's zapped at close range, there is one more ploy. If the driver immediately brakes, the radar will not lock in and produce a speed reading for the officer. Police radar does not record rapidly accelerating or decelerating vehicles, but only those travelling at a relatively steady speed. The problem with slamming on your brakes every time the detector beeps is that you may wind up with an 18-wheeler in your back seat!

The same microwave emissions that trigger false speed readings in police radar will cause false alarms in radar detectors. Experienced users of better quality radar detectors can soon tell the difference between Smokey and a microwave burglar alarm at the local bank.

If you don't want to invest in a detector, you may still be able to anticipate radar traps thanks to helpful motorists coming in the opposite direction. Flashing headlights (high-beams at night) are the signal that a radar trap lies ahead. If all the trucks you encounter are travelling at or below the speed limit, you're either going uphill or approaching a radar trap. Unexpected brake lights from traffic ahead may mean that other drivers have spotted Smokey in the bushes. Slow down!

# Radio Theft
How to keep those hits on board

Those forlorn "No Radio" signs in fancy cars are a shorthand message to thieves, asking them not to break a window in an attempt to steal a radio that has already been nabbed.

There are two kinds of anti-theft radios now available either from car makers, or from "aftermarket" suppliers—the latter for installation at car stereo stores. The most effective type plugs into a sleeve in the dashboard. It can be easily removed and taken with you whenever you park the car; most radios will fit into an attaché case or large purse. If you lock the radio in the trunk, you may lose it to thieves who break the trunk lock instead of a window.

The second type won't work once it has been removed from the car, unless you know a secret code number to punch into the radio keypad. A window decal explains this (though only to literate thieves). Most of these models have a little light that flashes whenever the ignition is off, to alert savvy felons that your radio has no resale value. This is a lot of knowledge to expect from a strung-out drug addict intent on converting your radio into another fix. Such radios may provide more revenge (after they are stolen) than protection. Better to take the radio with you.

# Rain
## How to drive safely in stormy weather

Accidents are twice as likely in the rain as on a dry day. The most dangerous time is when it first begins to rain after a dry spell. The first rainfall lifts accumulated oil and rubber from the pores of the pavement and brings this slippery stuff to the surface. After it has rained for a few hours, most of this slime is washed away.

Use all the controls gently when driving in the rain. Leave a larger margin than usual for emergencies and errors so you won't have to slam on the brakes, step on the gas, or wrench the steering wheel.

If you walk to your car in the rain, remember that your shoes are wet and might slip off the pedals. Wipe the soles of your shoes dry on the carpeting or floormats before you start the engine.

Good visibility is a must in bad weather. Use the defrosters (front and rear) if necessary to clear fog from inside the windows. Use the air conditioner on the recirculate setting (REC or MAX) in conjunction with the windshield defroster—the A/C's dehumidifying action will clear up fog faster than the heater's drying action. If you don't have air conditioning, make sure the defroster is *not* on the REC setting—you need fresh air to remove moisture from the car. You can wipe most of the moisture from the side windows by opening and closing them. Use paper towels to mop up excess water.

In light rain, use the MIST or INTERMITTENT wiper setting (if you have it) to avoid streaking the windshield. If it is already streaked, use the washer to clean the glass. Very little rain gets to the rear window at highway speeds; if the rear wiper has no intermittent setting, operate it in short bursts for the best results. Clean the wiper blades periodically with a paper towel and washer solution to remove road grime. If they still streak, smear, or chatter, replace them (see WINDSHIELD WIPERS).

In heavy rain, the faster you drive, the greater the amount of water hitting the windshield and the harder it is for the wipers to keep it clear. Decrease your speed accordingly.

Deep puddles can cause your tires to hydroplane—they'll climb up on the wet surface like water skis, losing contact with the road. When that happens, steering control is lost and you may spin out. If your steering suddenly feels light, the front tires are hydroplaning. Slow down until you regain steering control.

Water is squeezed out through the tread grooves as a tire rolls. The less tread you have on a tire, and the faster you drive, the more likely you are to hydroplane. Check the tread depth on your tires periodically and replace them before the depth reaches 1/16 inch (see TIRES).

# Rear Window Defroster
How to check and repair it

Rear window defrosters are required by law in some

northern states as a necessary piece of safety equipment. Actually, they are a good idea in any climate, since they clear fog as well as frost. They can be ordered as an option on a new car if they are not standard equipment. Paste-on defroster kits for used cars are available in auto parts stores.

Defrosters are a grid of thin wires that heat up when an electric current flows through them. They can evaporate moisture and melt small amounts of frost that block vision. They will not melt much snow.

If one of the wires is scratched or broken, electricity will not pass through it and that element will be unable to heat up and do its job. Never put decals or tape over the defroster wires; you are likely to damage them when these decorations are removed. When cleaning the inside of the rear window, use only a soft paper towel and liquid glass cleaner; never use abrasives or scrapers. Never rest hard objects that might scratch the wires against the window.

If you notice that one or more wires are not clearing fog from the glass, they are probably broken. Examine the wire(s) carefully to pinpoint the breaks. Use a magnifying glass if necessary. Auto parts stores sell defroster repair kits that contain a small bottle of electrically-conductive paint, a brush, and masking tape. Place bits of tape parallel to the wire, spanning the break. Then paint over the break. When the paint dries, the wire should work. If the entire grid is not working at all, check the fuse box (see FUSES).

## Recalls
Good intentions, mixed results

Car makers have been recalling vehicles to correct faults since at least 1914, when Buick replaced a defective leather hood strap as a goodwill gesture. But manufacturers have not always been so conscientious, and in 1966 the National Highway Traffic Safety Administration (NHTSA) stepped in to control recalls for safety-related defects, with mixed results. Under this program, more than 150 million cars have been recalled to fix potentially dangerous problems. However, some major ones have slipped by, including locking rear brakes on GM's "X" cars, and 21 million Ford-built cars with automatic transmissions alleged to slip from PARK into REVERSE while idling.

Manufacturers still recall cars voluntarily. Some of these defects, like rusting fenders on early Hondas, are not safety related, and the manufacturer may set a time limit for owners to respond. Safety recalls have no time limit. If the original owner did not have the problem corrected, a subsequent owner can, at no cost. Any dealer for that brand of car can do the work, not just the dealer who sold the car.

When shopping for a used car, call the NHTSA toll-free hotline (800-424-9393) to find out if that car model was involved in a recall. If it was, send the Vehicle Identification Number (VIN) to the manufacturer, who can tell you whether or not that particular car was repaired. If it wasn't, it is never too late to have the work done. The VIN is visible through the driver's side of the windshield, on a plate atop the dash; it also appears on your registration. For the car maker's address, see your Owner's Manual or CAR COMPANIES.

If you get a recall notice in the mail, call your dealer right away for an appointment to have the car inspected, and repaired if necessary. There may be a wait for the parts needed to fix a recalled car. If your car exhibits the problem that triggered the recall, tell the dealer you need to be put at the top of the list. If the problem is serious, do not drive the car until it has been repaired; ask for a loaner or rent a car.

Recalls for particularly gruesome defects tend to make newspaper headlines long before the manufacturer has devised a fix and distributed sufficient parts to the dealers. Don't call the dealer demanding a repair until you get your recall notice in the mail. Have the car inspected, and rent a car if you are uncomfortable driving yours.

For information on recalls about pollution control equipment, contact the Environmental Protection Agency; for all other non-safety recalls, contact the Federal Trade Commission (for addresses, see CONSUMER GROUPS).

# Recreation Vehicles
## Renting vs. buying

A recreation vehicle (RV) is a big investment, whether it is a motor home ($20,000-$50,000), van conversion ($15,000-$25,000), slide-in pickup truck camper (about $7000), travel trailer ($12,000-$15,000), or pop-up tent trailer (about $4000). In many cases, renting one for an annual vacation makes more sense than owning one and having to store and maintain it year-round, while suffering the depreciation on it.

For example, a 24-foot motorhome costs $200 to $600 a week to rent, depending on the location and season, while a 33-footer can run up to $1000 a week, plus 15 to 25 cents a mile. A van conversion averages $185 a week to rent plus 20 cents a mile. The Recreation Vehicle Rental Assn. (3251 Old Lee Highway, Fairfax, VA 22030) sells a directory of RV rental outlets. For information on RVs and RV vacations, write to the Recreation Vehicle Industry Association, Dept.

MB, P.O. Box 2999, Reston, VA 22090.

After renting several RVs of the type you're interested in, you'll be in a better position to decide which brand you would like to buy (if you think you want to own one). If you take your rental RV to campgrounds, compare notes with RV owners. Ask them frank questions about the pros and cons of their RVs, including service, insurance costs, and dealerships. RV financing is available from dealers, banks, and credit unions, just as it is for cars (see LOANS), although RV loans seldom have the bargain basement interest rates occasionally offered by car makers.

# Repair Costs
## How they're figured

The traditional method of calculating car repair costs is a great source of misunderstanding between consumers and repair shops. Most car dealers and independent garages estimate repair costs "by the book," using one of the standard estimating guides such as the *MOTOR Parts & Time Guide*. These books list the time it takes the *average* mechanic to perform a particular job on a particular car, as well as the retail prices for thousands of auto parts.

If you bring your car in for a new water pump, the shop can quickly determine the price of the part and the time required to do the job. Let's say the pump costs $75 and the job is listed at two hours for your car; if the shop charges $40 an hour, the estimate for your car would be $155 [$75 + (2 x $40)].

With a little luck, an experienced mechanic might be able to do the job in one-and-a-half hours. But most garages will stick to the original estimate, charging you the $155 and paying the mechanic for two hours' work.

The reasoning here is that other mechanics may be taking longer than the estimated time to do their jobs, and at the end of the day it pretty much averages out.

If your car had corroded parts that were hard to remove, or the mechanic broke a bolt, which then had to be drilled out, a conscientious shop would stick to its original estimate of two hours, even if the job took two and-a-half hours. (The mechanic would only be paid for the two "book hours," however.)

You should also understand that the mechanic receives only a fraction of the labor charge. The shop keeps the balance to pay for rent, utilities, equipment, insurance, taxes, employee benefits, and other overhead, plus its profit.

It would be more straightforward if shops simply charged a flat fee for each job—in the case above, $155 for the water pump—without breaking it down as to the cost of parts and labor. However, the parts/labor breakdown is such an ingrained tradition in the auto repair industry that most consumers insist on it. On some routine work, such as tuneups, brake work, and oil changes, many shops do use a fixed price, making no distinction between parts and labor.

Despite all this parts-vs.-labor confusion, the customer is always free to shop around for the lowest estimate before agreeing to have any work done.

In some large shops and in most car dealerships, you may see someone in a white coat filling out the work order—that's probably not a mechanic, but a sales person who gets a commission for selling service. That's why you should go in with a list of exactly what you want done, and try to stick to it (see REPAIRS).

# Repairs

Getting them done correctly

There is more to getting your car fixed right the first time than just finding a good mechanic (see MECHANICS), although that is the first step.

Good communication with the mechanic is the key to getting the job done properly. If you give the mechanic only a sketchy description of the problem, it's not likely to get fixed. Mechanics generally don't like to see a faulty job come back; a shop loses money when a "comeback" has to be fixed at no charge.

Before you go to the shop, make a list of any unusual problems, and exactly what you want done to the car in the way of routine maintenance. Write down all of the symptoms in as much detail as possible: How long has the condition existed? Is it constant or intermittent? Does it occur only under certain driving conditions? Is it accompanied by an unusual noise, vibration, or smell?

Make an appointment with the shop and explain the trouble at that time. Don't claim it's an emergency if the problem is just an annoyance. Good shops are busy and don't need customers who cry "Wolf!"

If possible, give your list of symptoms to the mechanic who will be working on your car. At a large dealership or garage, you may have to deal with a service writer—a sales person who gets a commission for selling service. Make sure your list is stapled to the work order, or else gets copied faithfully. "Check engine" is not an accurate description of a problem.

Try to stick to the symptoms and avoid your own diagnosis; mechanics are sometimes offended by "know-it-alls" who tell them to do one thing when the problem is something else. Some will perform the wrong job for spite.

Make sure all work is guaranteed, and that the guarantee is spelled out clearly on the work order or bill. Save the bill in case the work is faulty.

Keep a log book of all previous jobs, together with the work orders or bills, and refer the mechanic to it so work that has already been done is not repeated.

Ask for high and low "best-case, worst-case" estimates to be written on the work order. It is often impossible to diagnose a problem when the work order is written, and many garages guess high to avoid arguments later. If you OK the high estimate, they may be tempted to charge that amount no matter what the job cost. If the shop gives you just one estimate, ask how much it would cost "if the job doesn't turn out to be that complicated." Then ask them to call you if it appears the job will go above the low figure.

If you have taken a late-model car to a dealer to

cure a recurring problem, ask the dealer to look for a technical service bulletin (TSB) on the subject. Car makers issue TSBs each month to help cure specific problems, but few dealers read or file them properly (see TECHNICAL SERVICE BULLETINS).

Test drive the car as soon as you pick it up. If it hasn't been fixed, bring the car back right away. If the problem recurs, call the shop and ask for an immediate appointment. If they ask to be paid for additional work, ask for an adjustment on the original job, which apparently was not necessary. If you are not happy with their work, see COMPLAINTS.

## Rust
Keeping it under control

On today's modern unit-body cars, which do not have

a separate frame, rust is more than a cosmetic problem. Rusted out engine, transmission, and suspension mounts can lead to serious accidents. Road salt, used to melt ice and snow, is extremely corrosive to car parts.

The newest cars have extensive rustproofing built in at the factory, including the use of steel that's galvanized, coated with zinc-rich primers, or sprayed in hidden areas with waxy coatings. If you read the new car warranty, you may find that your car is guaranteed against "perforation" (rust-through) for three to seven years. Additional rustproofing, applied by car dealers or aftermarket concessions, is seldom necessary. In fact, it may undermine the factory rustproofing or void the warranty.

Do not confuse rustproofing with undercoating— the application of a tar-like substance to the bottom of the car. Undercoating reduces road noise, but it can trap water in cracks and accelerate rusting.

To prevent rust, wash the car often, especially in snow country winters when salty slush gets frozen in the wheel wells and underbody of the car. Wash the car often and hose out the wheel wells and underside. If you use a commercial car wash, pick one that sprays the underside of the car but doesn't recycle salt-laden water. If the car gets packed with ice, it is better to park it outside where the ice will stay frozen than to bring it into a heated garage where the ice will melt, leaving the salt behind. Salty water will rust a car faster than ice.

Unclog the drain holes along the bottoms of doors, in the trunk, and elsewhere to prevent moisture accumulation.

Repair paint damage immediately (see PAINT

TOUCH-UP). If your car needs major body work done, ask the body shop to apply factory-type rustproofing to the replacement parts.

# S

## Screws
### Big surprises in small packages

Just when you thought you had enough screwdrivers, you start to do a simple job on your car and find some bizarre fasteners you can't open. Here is a rundown of the five different screws you may come across. Each needs a special tool to open or tighten it.

*Slotted* screws are the standard type that you turn with a flat-blade screwdriver.

*Phillips-head* screws are turned with the familiar blunt-tip cross-blade screwdriver.

*Allen screws* require a hexagonal key called an Allen wrench. They are found on some dashboards and custom wheels. The tools needed for the three types of screws listed above are sold in various sizes at any good hardware store. Always use the right size driver, to avoid damaging the screw.

*Torx* fasteners have drive slots shaped like a six-pointed star. They are often used on car doorlocks, seatbelts, rearview mirrors, and body parts.

*Pozidriv* screws look like a Phillips screw with a square hole at the center of the cross slots. They are used on some headlight housings, doorlocks, and body parts. If you use a Phillips screwdriver on a Posidriv fastener, you'll strip it and won't be able to get it out. Pozidriv and Torx drivers are sold in different sizes at professional auto parts stores.

## Seatbelts
Fixing stuck ones

Modern combination lap/shoulder safety belts have inertia reels, which allow the belt to reel in and out freely for maximum comfort, but lock up if the car moves suddenly when braking, cornering, or in an accident.

Sometimes a twisted belt is reeled back into its housing where it gets stuck. The best fix is prevention—always keep the belt straight as it passes over loops and other guides. A twisted belt will put excess pressure on your body that may cause injury in an accident. Always keep belts flat across your lap and chest.

If a belt gets twisted and stuck in its housing, you can often free it by repeatedly pulling on the belt and releasing it, which will eventually work it loose. If you can't get it loose, bring the car to a dealer—it is difficult if not impossible to open seatbelt housings without special tools.

# Seatbelts, Passive
## The latest safety wrinkle

In an attempt to protect drivers, whether they want protection or not, a much-amended federal law requires that all cars be equipped with "passive restraints" by 1990 (though the law could be amended yet again). That means either air bags or passive seatbelts, which are designed to envelop the driver and front seat passenger with no action on their part. You will see passive seatbelts more frequently on new cars because they are cheaper than air bags.

There are two basic belt designs. The simplest ones are attached to the top and bottom of the front door. To get into the seat, you must slide under the belts, which rub against your body in an overly familiar fashion and snag on pencils, jewelry, large buttons, and other obstacles. When you close the door, the inertia reel pulls the belt snugly around you. Fortunately, you can use the "emergency" release at the center of the car like an ordinary seatbelt buckle to release the belts whenever you leave the car, and buckle them up before driving. This eliminates sliding under the belts, but also defeats the whole purpose of "passive" belts.

Motorized belts are a "Rube Goldberg" exercise perfected by the Japanese. The belt is attached to a track that runs around the door opening. When you close the door, a motor wraps the belt around you, often removing your hat or glasses in the process. This system includes only the shoulder belt; you must manually buckle the lap belt to prevent sliding under the shoulder belt in an accident and being strangled.

This is called progress.

# Sinking Car
## How to escape

If a car falls into a body of water, it may float for a short time before it sinks, motor first, toward the bottom. This is the time to escape, if you can, by opening a window and crawling out. When the car is partly submerged, it is hard to open the doors. If you have power windows or door locks, open them immediately, before the water shorts them out and makes them inoperative.

If the car is sinking quickly, close the windows to keep water from rushing in. Have everyone in the car take off their seatbelts and remove their shoes. Keep all heads above water as the level rises inside the car. You will not be able to open the doors against the water pressure until the car is almost full of water. When the water reaches your chin, tell everyone to take a deep breath, force open a door, and swim to the surface. Hold hands to form a chain so no one is lost or left behind.

If the car has fallen through ice, you will have to swim toward the hole the car made to reach the surface. Note that it is easy to get disoriented under the ice, especially if the car moves with the current while sinking. In addition to everything else, you must keep an eye on the escape hole through the windows as the car sinks. As soon as you reach shore, get medical treatment for exposure.

# Shock Absorbers
## How to know when they're shot

The British term for shock absorbers is "dampers," which is a more accurate description of what they do—damp the oscillating action of the springs so your car doesn't bound down the road like a Slinky toy. Good shocks also smooth out the ride and keep the tires firmly on the road, especially when cornering. Bad shocks do none of the above and are simply along for the ride. Cheap shocks, including the factory-installed models on many cars, act like worn-out shocks from Day One.

You can test the shocks on a parked car by repeatedly pushing down firmly on a fender or bumper until you have one corner of the car rocking up and down. Stop pushing and watch the car. If it continues to rock up and down more than once or twice, the shocks are no good.

A sensitive driver can evaluate the shocks while driving. Worn shocks cause the suspension to bottom out with a loud *thunk* on railroad crossings, bumps, or dips in the road, and the car will continue to pitch up and down with a boat-like motion long after hitting a bump.

Shocks should always be replaced in pairs (both fronts and/or both rears) to avoid lop-sided handling. When buying replacement shocks, always get top-line, heavy-duty models. You will be amazed at how much better your car handles and how secure you feel when cornering. Unless you own a sports car, avoid "high-performance" or racing shocks, which give a rough ride that will jar your teeth.

New shocks are particularly expensive for cars with MacPherson strut suspensions, because much of the suspension has to be disassembled and the springs removed to replace the shocks, so the labor charge is high. Top quality shocks are a must here—they will need changing far less often because they are made to last longer.

# Skid Control
Bring 'em back alive

Controlling a skid is a bit like riding a bicycle—it is basically a matter of "feel," balance, and experience. You must go out and practice it to get it right. This may sound crazy, but it's not a bad idea to practice skid control at low speeds in an empty parking lot that's covered with snow or ice—if you can do so without getting hurt or being arrested!

Several schools for race drivers and police have skid control courses. Check with your local police, or look at the classified ads in the back of a sports car magazine. Or, call your local high school and see if the Driver Ed instructor teaches skid control.

The theory of skid control is pretty basic—skids are caused by exceeding the traction limits of your tires when steering, braking, or accelerating. If your car starts to skid, you should stop whatever you are doing and try something else.

Most people know to lift off the gas pedal if the car's wheels start spinning. But few realize that you should do the same with the brake pedal: if the car starts to skid when you apply the brakes, reduce the pressure on the pedal, then try again. Gently pumping the brake pedal may avoid a skid. Stomping on the pedal in a panic will cause a skid and more than likely lost steering control, unless your car is equipped with an Anti-lock Brake System (ABS), which uses a computer to pump the brakes automatically (see BRAKES, ANTI-LOCK).

Controlling a skid in a turn is more difficult, because you often have no room for corrective maneuvers, which could take the car through a wider arc. If the back of the car begins to slide out to one side, keep your feet off both the gas and the brakes, and steer in the direction of the skid—to the left if the rear end is sliding to the left, and likewise for the right. When the car has straightened out, try again to gently steer in the direction you want to go. Often, when you correct a skid in one direction, the car will try to skid in the other direction. Be prepared to steer quickly back and forth several times if the car "fish-tails" from side to side.

Sometimes, a car will skid straight ahead when you want it to turn. This often happens when braking. Reduce pressure on the brake pedal, straighten the wheel slightly, then try to gently steer in the direction you want to go. Pump the brake pedal on and off if necessary to regain steering control.

If you are going too fast for the road conditions,

none of these corrective actions will work. The trick is to avoid a skid in the first place by noting the condition of the road surface and driving accordingly. A curve that is safe at 50 mph dry may be dangerous at 45 mph wet, at 35 mph in the snow, and at 15 mph if it's icy. Avoiding skids is a matter of "reading" the road conditions ahead, having a feel for your car's handling, and using common sense. Don't simply slow to a snail's pace in bad weather, or you may be involved in an accident caused by an impatient driver trying to pass.

## Snow Tires
How much snow do you want to go through?

All tire designs are a compromise between features that work better on some surfaces than on others— mud, snow, ice, dry pavement or wet, etc. What you gain in one area is often lost in the others.

Most tires sold today are radials, but there are many types available for different seasons and different purposes—high-performance tires, mud/snow tires, all-season tires, studded tires, and conventional tires. The kind of winter tires you need depends on the weather in your area and how badly you have to get somewhere when road conditions are bad.

Owners of sporty cars with high-performance tires are often embarrassed to find that they can't get out of their own driveways when it snows. Most high-performance tires are single-purpose designs that work best only on a dry, smooth road.

Conventional radials are little better than high-performance tires on snow. Mud/snow tires are best in deep, unplowed snow, but, surprisingly, they are not as good as all-season tires on plowed snow or slush—the kind of snow most people encounter (see Chart A).

Studded snow tires have little advantage in snow, but can be a life-saver on ice (see Chart B). Because they damage dry roads, studs are illegal in some states and are restricted to the winter months in others. Contact your local police or Department of Motor Vehicles for details.

If you don't get a lot of snow where you live (or don't have to go out in it), all-season radials should be just fine, and you won't have to worry about swapping tires twice a year. A new type of all-season high performance tire works well in snow and rain, while still giving exceptional traction on dry roads. It is probably the safest tire you can put on any car. Unfortunately, these tires are very expensive and don't have the tread life of conventional radials.

If you often have to drive in deep snow, there is no substitute for mud/snow tires, preferably with studs. You should have them mounted on an extra set of wheels so they can be installed and removed without taking them on and off the rims, which can damage the tire beads.

Snow tires should be used on all four wheels of most cars to equalize traction all around. On a rear-drive car, the front wheels do most of the braking and all of the steering. If they don't have as much traction as the driven wheels, you are likely to slide off a snowy road nose first. Makers of front-drive cars usually insist on snow tires for all four wheels, too. That's because it is easy to lock up the rear wheels of a nose-heavy front-drive car and spin out when braking if all four wheels don't have equal traction.

Chains give the best traction on snow and ice, but they are difficult to install and must be removed when you reach clear pavement or when driving at highway speeds; otherwise they will damage your tires.

SNOW TIRES, CHART A

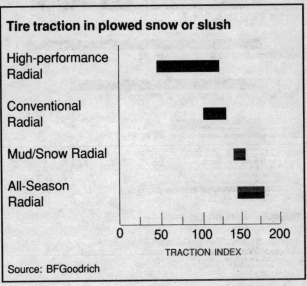

**Tire traction in plowed snow or slush**

High-performance Radial

Conventional Radial

Mud/Snow Radial

All-Season Radial

TRACTION INDEX

Source: BFGoodrich

SNOW TIRES, CHART B

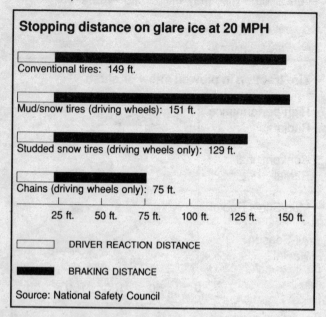

**Stopping distance on glare ice at 20 MPH**

Conventional tires: 149 ft.

Mud/snow tires (driving wheels): 151 ft.

Studded snow tires (driving wheels only): 129 ft.

Chains (driving wheels only): 75 ft.

| 25 ft. | 50 ft. | 75 ft. | 100 ft. | 125 ft. | 150 ft. |

☐ DRIVER REACTION DISTANCE

■ BRAKING DISTANCE

Source: National Safety Council

# Speeding Tickets
## How to beat them

Surveys show that most drivers want to have speeders ticketed, but are outraged when they themselves are stopped. In many areas, traffic routinely moves along at 10 to 15 mph above the posted limit, and drivers who get tickets feel that they have been singled out unfairly.

The best defense is a good radar detector, which warns you of radar surveillance in time for you to slow down and let someone else get the ticket. An increasingly unpopular alternative is to obey the law. Or, you can listen to CB radio reports of where Smokey is "taking pictures" (using radar) or patrolling. Checking your mirrors often is a good safety habit that also lets you spot cops sneaking up behind you.

If, despite all this, you are stopped for speeding, be polite (see POLICE), but look for loopholes in the officer's procedure. If radar was used, ask if it was K-band (short range) or X-band (long range). This will at least make you sound knowledgeable and interested in police work.

Ask how your car was determined to be the speeding one (see RADAR DETECTORS). If the answer is you were the first in an approaching group, which is likely, ask about that other car (be specific about its make and model) that was speeding up behind you, but slammed on the brakes when its driver saw the officer. Surely that was the one that triggered the radar. Let the officer know, politely, that you are prepared to go to court to question the procedures used in this incident. If you are up against a hard-nosed cop filling a quota, nothing you say will save you. But if the officer is reasonable and would rather not waste a day in a stuffy courtroom, you may be let go in favor of easier game.

If the trooper paced you from behind and clocked you on a calibrated speedometer, shame on you for not noticing! But you still may get off on a technicality if you were not paced for the distance prescribed by state law (a good reason to know your local laws). I once wormed my way out of a ticket because the pursuing officer never matched my speed. I was accelerating when he took off after me, but I immediately braked to a halt; it was impossible to pace me.

Sometimes a sense of humor will save the day. A friend has been let go several times when troopers couldn't keep a straight face after noting that he had listed one of his private parts in the organ donor section of his driver's license. And there's still something to be said for a tight sweater on a woman equipped to flaunt it. But forget the lame excuses—they are an admission of guilt, and the cops have heard them all. In fact, they collect the outrageous ones for locker room bull sessions.

Many states assign points to your license for moving violations, then suspend the license if you collect enough points. In some states, you can take points off your license and/or reduce the cost of auto insurance by taking a state-approved accident prevention course. Ask your state Department of Motor Vehicles for details.

# Steering Failure
## Now what?

Total loss of steering control—when you turn the wheel and nothing happens—is rare. The most common causes are skidding on ice and hydroplaning in deep water (see RAIN). When your tires cannot grip the road, all steering control is lost. To avoid skids, slow to a safe speed when road conditions are bad. To control a skid that has already begun, see SKID CONTROL.

Loss of steering, aside from skids, is caused when a part in the steering linkage breaks. The best you can do is apply the brakes firmly, but not too hard—panic braking may throw the car into a skid. Blow your horn and put on your bright lights and emergency flashers to warn other drivers. Call for a tow truck.

An apparent loss of steering is much more common, and most often caused by a failure in the power steering system. This will reduce or eliminate the power assist, but you should still be able to steer the car with extra effort. The wheel will be hard to turn—like a truck—especially at lower speeds. The natural adrenaline rush of panic will help you to strong-arm the wheel at higher speeds.

It will be even harder to turn the wheel when the car has stopped. Use the technique known to drivers of cars without power steering—move the car forward or backward slightly as you turn the wheel. This will take less effort.

Power assist may be lost for several reasons: (1) a stalled engine; (2) a loose or broken drive belt on the power steering pump; (3) low power steering fluid level.

You can tell if your engine has stalled by checking the instrument panel. The tachometer and oil pressure gauges (if you have them) will drop to zero. The ALTERNATOR, CHARGE, OIL PRESSURE, and/or ENGINE warning lights will come on.

If the road is straight and empty, you may be able to restart the engine while the car is coasting. Shift into NEUTRAL and turn the ignition key to the START position. (But be sure the engine has actually stalled—if you engage the starter while the engine is running, expensive damage may result!)

If the engine doesn't restart immediately, try to coast to a safe spot on the shoulder or well off the road and then stop. When the engine has stalled, power assist to the brakes will also diminish; slow almost to a stop before you pull off the road. Then try to restart the engine after coming to a complete stop.

If the engine hasn't stalled, drive carefully to a place where it is safe to stop the car well off the road. Turn off the engine and open the hood. Being careful not to get burned on hot engine parts, locate the power steering pump. Check the fluid level and add more fluid if necessary (see POWER STEERING FLUID). As soon as possible, have a mechanic check the system for leaks. Meanwhile, check the fluid often until you can get the car to a mechanic.

If the power steering pump's drive belt is loose or broken, tighten or replace it (see BELTS).

If you can't find and fix the problem at the side of the road, drive slowly and carefully to the nearest service station, or have the car towed.

## Steering Shimmy
### When your wheel gets spastic

Steering wheel vibration can be caused by worn parts in the suspension or steering linkage, misaligned wheels, out-of-balance tires, or a warped disc brake. All four conditions require professional attention, but an out-of-balance tire is the cheapest to fix. If you can't get to a tire store or garage immediately, switching an out-of-balance tire to the rear of the car will mask the condition.

If the shimmy occurs only during light braking, it's probably from a warped front disc brake. Sometimes this can be fixed by having the disc ground, rather than replacing it.

Faulty wheel alignment is relatively easy to fix on rear-drive cars, because only the front wheels need to be adjusted. Front-drive cars often require alignment of all four wheels, not just the front pair.

Several tire problems can also cause shimmy. They include improper inflation (which you can fix yourself—see TIRE PRESSURE), uneven tread wear, or the mixing of different tire sizes or types.

## Stuck in Mud, Sand, or Snow
How to get going again

If your car loses traction and starts to spin its wheels in mud, sand, or snow, don't stand on the gas and try to bull your way out—you'll only spin the wheels more and dig yourself in deeper. Try to gently rock the car out by shifting back and forth between DRIVE and REVERSE on automatic transmissions, and FIRST and REVERSE on manual transmissions. Keep the front wheels pointed straight ahead, if possible, for the least resistance.

Successful rocking requires a definite rhythm and feel. Apply as little gas as possible to help keep the wheels from spinning. As the car begins to climb up the sides of the hole its wheels have dug, time each shift so it occurs at the high point of each rock; this will increase your momentum and the chances of getting out of the hole.

Don't overdo it. If you're not free after a dozen rocks, try something else. Excessive rocking can overheat and damage an automatic transmission. If you cannot rock the car free, and don't want to attempt the strenuous methods described below, now is the time to call for a tow truck. Otherwise:

You can increase the traction of a rear-drive vehicle by placing more weight over the rear wheels: put all of your passengers into the rear seats, or load the trunk with plastic garbage bags filled with snow, sand or rocks.

Although it's a bit late, now is a good time to install snow chains—if you have them and can get them onto the stuck wheels.

Use your hands or a shovel to dig ramps through sand or snow down to the bottom of the stuck wheels. A long, shallow ramp is easier to climb than the sides of the hole.

If you can jack the car up safely, fill in the holes and place some carpet, wood, metal mesh, or other traction aid under the stuck tire(s). Do this only if you can dig down to firm ground to support the jack. Lower the car onto the traction aid and remove the jack. Have any helpers stand well clear of the car when you try to drive off; traction aids can fly out if the wheels begin to spin, causing injury or death to bystanders.

A ratchet-type engine hoist, "come-along," or block and tackle can also be attached to a strong tree and used to winch a stuck car onto firm ground. This is a pleasant theory, but it requires a lot of foresight to carry the winch and sufficient chain or rope in your car.

# Technical Service Bulletins
The key to good dealer service

The service engineers at car companies spend their time figuring out the best way to work on new cars. They write the service manuals that mechanics refer to, and try to solve problems that crop up in the field. When the company receives reports of a wide-spread problem, the service engineers work out a repair and issue a Technical Service Bulletin (TSB) to their dealers. The TSB will list the correct repair procedure and, often, the part number of redesigned components developed to cure the problem.

This is all wonderful, except that many dealership mechanics and service managers never read or properly file their TSBs, so they can't find the information when they need it, or else are completely unaware that a special fix exists. For example, a shop may be wasting its time adjusting and rebuilding a carburetor to correct a driveability problem like bucking or hesitation, while an unread TSB in a ring binder up on the shelf would tell the mechanic that the problem is really a malfunctioning shift valve in the automatic transmission.

When the shop replaces perfectly good parts under warranty, they are returned to the manufacturer for inspection. If the parts are found to be good, the car maker won't reimburse the dealer for the work. So when you bring your car back with the same old problem, the dealer is mad at *you*. He may tell you "They're all like that," (which is certainly true as far as the cars leaving his shop are concerned) and that he can't fix it.

If the dealer seems baffled by a problem with a late-model car, ask if they have received a TSB on the subject. If the answer is "no," ask to see their TSB file so you can help locate it. If your request is refused, or the file is a hopeless mess, you will have to get the information elsewhere, or try a better-organized dealership.

If you can get the *number and date* of the TSB that deals with your car's problem, most dealers will manage to look it up. The problem here is that car makers tend to view TSBs as top-secret documents. First try the service rep at your car maker's Zone Office (you can get the number from the dealer or your Owner's Manual). You can get Ford, Lincoln, and Mercury TSBs by calling 800-241-FORD; and GM TSBs from the dealer, or by calling 800-551-4123. GM indexes are free, but there is a charge for the TSBs.

The National Highway Traffic Safety Administration has safety-related TSBs on file. To get copies, write to NHTSA, Technical Reference Division, NAD-52, Room 5109, 400 7th St. SW, Washington, DC 20590, providing the make, model, and year of the car, plus the malfunctioning component (steering, brakes, etc.). A computer search of NHTSA's files will generate a list of TSBs, and you can then request copies from the list. There are fees for staff time, computer time, and copying, all of which must be paid in advance. For more detailed information, call the Division at (202) 366-2768.

# Theft Alarms
## Make your car a tough case for crooks

There are lots of burglar alarms and anti-theft devices on the market, such as steering and transmission locks. Some are more useful than others. Those big steel rods with a hook on each end that lock the steering wheel to the brake pedal look great, but an experienced thief can simply saw a piece out of the steering wheel and the lock will fall to the floor. Such gizmos may deter an amateur thief, but they will not prevent someone from smashing a window to steal the radio or other valuables like radar detectors that have been left in sight.

A good anti-theft alarm is the best protection against thieves, particularly amateurs, who are responsible for 70% of all stolen cars. Police say that if a pro wants your car, he'll get it one way or another, even if he has to disable the battery and tow it away. Some thieves will purposely trigger an alarm, then hide while you reset it. After a few times, most owners assume it's malfunctioning and turn it off. Next day, no car. A good alarm together with a second device, like a fuel or ignition cutoff, gives the best protection.

An effective alarm should set off a siren (not just the car horn) and flash the lights (so bystanders can tell which car is sounding off in a crowded parking lot). It should turn itself off and re-arm after two to five minutes so it doesn't drain the battery. Radio thieves will often rip a radio from the dash while the alarm is blaring and run off. If that's a problem in the area where you must park, consider a painfully loud siren *inside* the car (just don't trigger it by accident while you're inside!).

Any number of sensors are used on different systems to set off the siren. More expensive alarms allow you to choose combinations of sensors to customize your system. Any alarm should go off when a door, trunk, or hood is opened. Motion detectors trigger the siren if the car is towed (or bumped by a parking car, which is why you need an automatic shutoff and re-arm feature). A sound discriminator is a microphone that can tell breaking glass from a passing truck. An ultrasonic sensor can detect motion inside the car (it should be adjustable so it won't go off for house flies!). A pressure sensor detects the weight of someone in the driver's seat.

A remote alarm has a small sending unit you can put on your key ring to arm or disarm the system from outside the car. This allows you to open the trunk or a passenger door, without first getting into the driver's side to disarm the system. Many also have a "panic button" so that you can set off the siren if you're assaulted near the car or while entering it.

A window decal for warning off thieves is a good idea, but it should not mention the brand name, which tells a pro how your system works.

# Tire Changing
### Easy when you know how

Tire changing is a basic skill that every driver should have in case of a flat, to swap snow tires for summer ones, or to rotate the tires periodically. There's a bit more to it than meets the eye, but with the tips below all but the frailest individual can do it.

1) Park on firm, level ground well off the road. Remove the jack and spare tire from the trunk. Use the tapered end of the jack handle or a big screwdriver to pry the hub cap (if any) off the wheel to expose the lug nuts. If the car has a special tool for removing expensive wire wheel covers, follow the instructions packed with the tool.

2) Use the lug wrench to loosen the lug nuts before you raise the car. On most cars, you turn them counter-clockwise. They should be marked if they loosen clockwise. If the nuts are too tight, use your foot to push down on the wrench; or, steady yourself on a fender and stand on the wrench. Bounce a little if necessary, but be careful not to slip off the wrench!

3) Raise the car at the jacking point nearest the tire to be changed (see JACKING IT UP). Raise the car until the tire is an inch above the ground (three to four inches for flats).

4) Make sure the car sits firmly on the jack. Then remove the lug nuts and wheel. Put the lug nuts in a clean, safe place—inside the hub cap is handy.

5) Hang the replacement wheel onto the wheel

studs. Make sure the correct side of the wheel is facing out, and that the mounting holes in the wheel are aligned with the studs before you lift the wheel. If it feels heavy, wedge your toes under the tire and lift it with your leg muscles.

6) When you hang the wheel on the studs, it may swing outward at the bottom. Push the wheel flat against its mounting surface and screw on the lug nuts by hand, starting at the bottom. The tapered side of each nut must face the wheel. When the nuts are fin-ger-tight, use the lug wrench to gently snug up the nuts—don't exert too much pressure or you may knock the car off the jack.

7) When the wheel is on straight and snug, lower the car to the ground and remove the jack. Now use the wrench to make the nuts as tight as possible, work-ing in a criss-cross pattern to avoid tightening any two adjacent nuts, which can crack the wheel.

8) If this is an emergency roadside repair, just toss the flat, jack, and hubcap into the trunk, remove the wheel chocks, and drive to a safer spot. Then secure the jack properly, refit the hub cap, and have the flat fixed if possible (see TIRE REPLACEMENT).

# Tire Pressure
## How to check and adjust it

Incorrect pressure is the most common cause of tire failure. Tires with too little air will flex too much on the highway, generating excess heat that can cause a blowout. They will also increase fuel consumption, reduce cornering power, wear out first at the edges, and may squeal when you round a corner at normal speeds.

Tires with too much air will give a harsh ride and wear out first at the center. Uneven pressure from one tire to another may cause the car to pull to one side, shimmy, or handle oddly.

Check your tire pressure at least once a month and before long trips. Do this with an accurate pressure gauge. Don't rely on the gauge at a gas station's air pump—they are often inaccurate. To use the gauge, unscrew the cap on the end of the tire valve and press the gauge firmly onto the valve stem so that no air leaks out. Some wheels with fancy wheel covers have an extended cap with a white dot in the center. This dot is a spring-loaded valve, which means you can take pressure readings and add air through this cap without removing it.

Remove the gauge and read the pressure on the scale. Check all five tires, including the spare, when the tires are cold (pressure can increase by six psi or more when the tires are hot from driving). First thing in the morning is a good time, or when you have been off the road for at least three hours. The correct pressure is listed on a label attached to the driver's door. If the tires are low, drive slowly to the nearest gas station and add air. Never "bleed" excess air from a hot tire; it will be underinflated when it cools down.

To use the type of air pump shown in the illustration, turn the handle on the side until the desired pressure appears in the window. Then press the air hose nozzle firmly against the valve stem until air stops flowing and the bell stops ringing. Double check the pressure with your pocket gauge. For other types of air pumps, add air a little at a time and check the pressure with your gauge.

If one tire loses pressure slowly and there is no obvious leak (like a nail or piece of glass in the tread), have the gas station remove the wheel and check the tire, valve, and wheel for leaks. If all your tires lose pressure slowly, this may be normal for some types of tire. If they are down five psi every time you take a reading, then check them more often.

## Tire Replacement
### When to throw in the towel

Some flats cannot be fixed. Driving any distance on a flat tire can damage the sidewalls beyond repair. If a radial tire has a puncture in the sidewall, it's a goner, no matter how much tread is left. Tubeless tires are usually repaired by inserting a rubber plug into a puncture. If the hole is too big to fix with one plug, replace the tire; multiple plugs will distort the tread and lead to internal failure. If the tires have a road hazard guarantee, the tire maker may reimburse all or part of the replacement cost.

Tires should be replaced well before they are completely bald. Bald tires will skid in even a drizzle, and tires with badly worn treads can hydroplane in puddles (see RAIN). A tread depth of 1/16 inch or less is unsafe, and illegal in most states. You can measure the tread depth by sticking the edge of a penny into the tread grooves head first. If you can see the top of Lincoln's hair, replace the tire.

Check all the grooves across the tire to see if they are wearing faster in one area than another. Excess wear on the outer edges means the tires are underinflated or you corner like a race driver. Excess wear down the middle means the tires are overinflated. Low tread in just one spot is caused by skidding on dry pavement or by an out-of-balance tire. An irregular pattern of low spots may be due to faulty wheel alignment, bad shocks, or an out-of-balance tire.

Wear bars (slightly raised areas) are cast into the tire tread at regular intervals. When the tread wears down to 1/16 inch, these bars will appear as gaps in the tread. If the wear bars appear between two or more adjacent tread grooves, it's time for new tires.

When you replace tires, make sure that both tires on the same axle are identical or at least closely matched. Tires of different size, construction, or radically different tread pattern will have different steering, braking, and traction behavior. This may lead to spooky handling. Radial tires should never be mixed with other types.

High-performance all-season tires give the greatest safety margin in all weather, but are very expensive and do not wear well. Tires with the longest tread life are made from very hard rubber that doesn't grip the road well in emergency maneuvers. All-season tires are a good compromise for year-round driving (see SNOW TIRES).

# Tire Rotation
Getting the most from your rubber

Rotating your tires periodically will not necessarily make them last longer, but it will equalize wear on all four or five tires so they all wear out at about the same time. This is a good idea because, by the time you wear out a set of tires, there are likely to be new designs on the market that you will want for all four wheels.

Tire makers have changed their minds about tire rotation several times over the last few years, and they may do so again. The latest word is that you should rotate the tires from wheel to wheel every 6000 to 8000 miles. If you change to snow tires in the winter, mark the tires you remove with chalk to show which wheel they were on. (Mark them RF, LF, RR, LR). That way, you can rotate the tires when you reinstall them. Store unused tires on their sides (lying flat) in a cool, dry place.

To rotate tires, move the rear tires straight to the front on each side of the car. Cross-switch the front tires, moving the left front (LF) tire to the right rear (RR) and the right front (RF) to the left rear (LR). If you have a full-size spare tire with good tread, you might move it to the right rear and put the left front tire into the trunk. *Do not* include a temporary-use spare in the tire rotation pattern!

## Tools to Go
### What to carry for emergencies

Some cars come with tool kits for emergency use on the road. Even if you don't know how to repair a car yourself, if you have the right tools along, a knowledgeable passerby may be able to make a simple repair to get you going again. You should also carry some extra fluids (but not gasoline, which is explosive). Here's what to carry:

Antifreeze (or 50/50 coolant mix)
Blanket (woven or "space" type)
Brake fluid (new, unopened can)
Coveralls
Spare drive belt(s)
Fire extinguisher
First aid kit
Flashlight
Flares
Spare fuses
Hand cleaner in foil packs or a tube
Spare hose clamp and silver duct tape
Ice scraper
Small lockback knife
Spare light bulbs
Motor oil
Plastic bags
Plastic raincoat
Locking pliers
Screwdrivers (flat blade and Phillips head)
Spare spark plugs and plug wrench
Spark plug cable (the longest one used on your
    car).
Paper towels
Collapsible umbrella
Adjustable water pump pliers
Water
Wide board to put under jack on soft ground
Wheel chocks
Spare wiper blades
Wrench set (adjustable wrenches are too big to
    fit into many tight spots around the car)

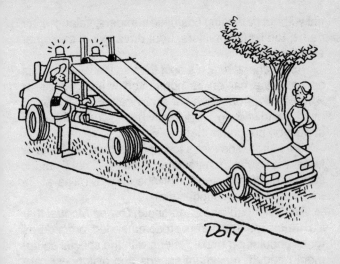

# Tow Trucks
## More harm than good?

The traditional "wrecker" with its sling and hook is *not* recommended for towing many modern cars. Front-wheel drive and aerodynamic designs with their air dams and plastic-covered bumpers often cannot be towed in the traditional way without damage. For these cars, you need new types of equipment: an "eagle claw" wheel-lift device that slides under the car, grabs the tires, and lifts them off the ground; or a flat-bed trailer—a truck with a tilting bed that tips up like a dump truck. The car is winched up onto the tilted bed, then lowered to a horizontal position and driven away with all four wheels off the ground.

Even older cars that can be towed with a hook require the expert use of such extra equipment as safety chains, J-hooks, T-hooks, grab hooks, wooden spacer blocks, and/or lengths of 4x4 lumber to lift and tow a car without damaging cosmetic bumpers, valances, air dams, fog lights, mufflers, front-drive axles, and other equipment.

As a general rule, it's best to raise the drive wheels and tow the car on its non-driven wheels (the rear wheels on a front-drive car and vice versa). If the car must be towed on its driven wheels, a special dolly should be put under them.

Cars should never be towed more than 50 miles, or faster than 50 mph; many manufacturers specify much shorter distances and lower speeds (15 miles at 25 mph is a common suggestion).

The AAA publishes an annual *Towing Manual* that illustrates manufacturers' recommended procedures for all popular car makes, along with the special equipment needed, maximum speeds and distances, cautions, warnings, and notes. No one can memorize all this stuff, and it's not covered thoroughly in some Owner's Manuals. Whoever tows your car should have a copy of this AAA guidebook.

Unless you subscribe to a road service program (see EMERGENCY ROAD SERVICE), you are pretty much at the mercy of the tow truck operator, as far as price goes. Most operators accept only cash, so be sure you agree on a rate before your car goes "on the hook." Demand a receipt so you can be reimbursed by your insurance company (if you have such coverage). Be suspicious of an operator who will tow you only to his shop, even if your preferred garage is nearby.

## Trailer Towing
How to keep the tail from wagging the dog

If there's anything spookier than trying to follow or pass a trailer that's swaying and wandering all over the road, it's trying to tow that trailer! Here's how to do it right:

For starters, the tow vehicle (car, van, or truck) should be equipped with a special package of towing equipment, available as an option on new vehicles that are suitable for towing, or as "aftermarket" equipment that can be installed on used cars. The towing package should include a heavy-duty cooling system, brakes, suspension, and electrical system, plus an engine oil cooler and transmission fluid cooler (the latter is for automatics, which are best for towing).

Check your Owner's Manual to find out the towing limits for your car or truck. Many newer vehicles—especially those with front-drive—are not recommended for towing at all. Using them to tow a trailer can void your warranty or service contract.

Next, get the right trailer hitch for the load you want to tow. Today's lightweight cars with their plastic bumpers and unit-body construction (no separate frame) defy the use of traditional bumper hitches. If you can fit a hitch at all, it may be a complex affair that needs to be welded to the unit-body platform in several places.

Hitches are rated by the total trailer weight they can tow, and the "tongue weight" (the tongue being the trailer extension) they can carry on the hitch ball: Class I (2000-lb. trailer weight, 200-lb. tongue weight); Class II (3500/350 lbs.); Class III (5000/500 lbs.); and Class IV (over 5000 lbs., which requires a hefty truck with special equipment). A load-equalizing or weight-distribution hitch transfers some of the trailer weight forward so that the back of the car doesn't drag and the front wheels don't lose traction.

Load the trailer so that heavy items are at the bottom, and concentrated over or slightly forward of the axle. If too much weight is in the rear, the trailer tongue will pull up on the hitch instead of pressing down, thus making the car unstable. You can measure the tongue weight of lighter trailers with a bathroom scale as you load them. For heavier trailers, rest the trailer tongue on a piece of heavy lumber across two bathroom scales and total the two weights.

Never tow at speeds greater than 50 mph. Allow twice your normal stopping distance and at least that much extra room for passing. Shift into lower gears (or at least out of *Overdrive* on four-speed automatics) when climbing or going downhill. Use the brakes sparingly on long downhill runs to avoid overheating and fading. Change engine oil and transmission fluid and perform other maintenance more frequently on a tow vehicle (see your Owner's Manual). Check all fluid levels, tire pressures, hitch, and trailer lights before each day's trip. Otherwise, have a good time!

One of the most difficult driving skills with a trailer is backing it into a parking space. Here's a simple rule of thumb to follow: Place your hand at the top of the steering wheel when backing up. To make the trailer go to the left, move your hand to the right. To make the trailer go right, move your hand left.

## Transmission Fluid
How to check it and add more

Once a month, you should check the fluid level in your automatic transmission. The transmission has a dipstick, much like the one for the engine (see OIL LEVEL). The level should be checked with the engine running and the transmission at operating temperature (after driving 20 minutes or more). Park the car on level ground, move the shift lever through all its positions, then apply the parking brake and put the transmission into NEUTRAL or PARK (see your Owner's Manual).

Open the hood and, being careful not to touch moving or hot parts, remove the transmission dipstick. Wipe the dipstick with a paper towel, then reinsert it into the dipstick tube and remove it again. Check the level of fluid clinging to it. If the transmission is at operating temperature, the fluid should be between the FULL and ADD marks.

If the level is below the ADD mark, add fluid one pint at a time until the dipstick reads FULL. Use the type of fluid specified in your Owner's Manual (there are several types of transmission fluid…use of the wrong one can damage the transmission). Fluid is added through the dipstick hole using a funnel. If you prefer, have a competent gas station attendant add the fluid.

Fresh transmission fluid is red or pink. If the fluid clinging to the dipstick is brown or black, or smells burned, the transmission needs service; at the very least, the fluid and transmission filter should be changed. Burned, gritty fluid may mean that a transmission rebuild is needed. As a precaution, you should have the fluid and filter changed every three to four years.

# Trim
## Keeping it all together

In the old days, car trim, including model names, side rub strips, and other decorations were screwed onto the bodywork or held on by fasteners that fit through holes drilled into the body. These mounting methods tended to promote rust. Today, much trim is held on by adhesives and may peel off in time. You can reglue loose trim with special trim adhesive or weatherstrip adhesive sold in auto parts stores, or with an instant-setting cement.

First, remove any old adhesive from the body and trim. Then clean both areas with a 50/50 mixture of water and rubbing alcohol. For best results, the car body should be between 70 and 125 degrees. If necessary, heat the trim and bodywork with a hair dryer.

Position the trim before gluing, to be sure it will fit properly. Then apply the adhesive, following the package directions, and press the trim into place. Allow the adhesive to set and don't wash the car for several days.

# Turbochargers
The power option

Many new car models are offered with turbochargers, an option that boosts engine power dramatically, and can give a four-or six-cylinder car the performance of a V8. The turbo is a small, turbine-type pump that is driven by the engine's exhaust gas and acts like a supercharger. It forces more air and fuel into the cylinders than they would ordinarily accept, which in turn produces more power. That's the good news.

The bad news about turbochargers is that they put extra strain on the engine and thus shorten engine life. Some car makers have started to limit their number of turbo models, now that six- and seven-year warranties are being offered. The turbo itself is also prone to trouble because it operates at very high temperatures, and at speeds of over 100,000 rpm.

Large volumes of smoke from the tailpipe, or a high-pitched whining noise accompanied by a loss of power, signals turbo failure. Have the engine checked as soon as possible.

For maximum turbo life, you must change engine oil frequently (every 2000 to 3000 miles—see your Owner's Manual). You should also let the engine idle for at least 30 seconds before turning it off; this allows the turbo to slow down to its idle speed before the engine's oil pump turns off.

A turbo option can add more than $1000 to the price of a car because it is usually packaged with better tires, brakes, and suspension to handle the extra power. Most turbocharged engines are a bit peculiar to drive, due to a phenomenon called "turbo lag." From the time you step on the gas, there is a few seconds' delay before the extra power of the turbo is felt. Then suddenly the power comes on with a great rush that some drivers appreciate, but others find disconcerting. However, an automatic transmission masks this lag somewhat.

# Turn Signals
## Fixing a bad flasher

Your turn signals are controlled by a switch on the steering column, and by a flasher unit under the dash. This small cylindrical or rectangular unit contains a resistance wire that heats up when electrical current flows through it and expands, breaking the contact so the lights go out. When this happens, the wire cools and contracts, making contact again and causing the turn signals to light up again. The process is repeated until the driver either turns off the signal switch, or turns the steering wheel back to the straight-ahead position.

The switch on the steering column rarely fails. Most problems with turn signals are caused by burned-out bulbs or flasher units. If a bulb burns out, the flasher will work faster than usual. Check the lights all around the car with the left signal on, and then the right. If one bulb doesn't flash, replace it (see BULB REPLACEMENT).

If none of the lights flash, the flasher is burned out. Check under the dash for the cylindrical flasher unit, which may be mounted in the fuse block (see FUSES) or by itself. Most cars have two of them—one is for the turn signals, the other for the hazard warning lights. On some imported cars, the fuse box and flashers are mounted under the hood, and the flasher may be rectangular.

Unplug the flasher and take it to an auto parts store to be sure you get an identical replacement. Plug in the replacement and you should be back in business. If not, the switch on the steering column may be bad. Save the original flasher as a spare and have a mechanic check the switch.

## Under-hood Checks

Things the pump jockey (often) won't tell you

The advent of self-service gas stations and kids manning the pumps elsewhere means that most people no longer enjoy the luxury of an experienced hand checking under the hood each time they pull in for gas. That means you must do it yourself, either at the gas station or, better yet, in the relative privacy of your own driveway, where you can take time to do it right. Carmakers have made this job easier by making many fluid reservoirs and some batteries of translucent plastic, so you can check their fluid levels without opening them. Here are the things to check:

- Engine oil level (see OIL LEVEL)
- Battery electrolyte level (see BATTERY)
- Drive belt tension and condition (see BELTS)
- Brake fluid level (see BRAKE FLUID)
- Power steering fluid level (see POWER STEER-ING FLUID)
- Radiator coolant level (see OVERHEATING)
- Windshield washer fluid level: If the reservoir is low, add a premixed washer solution, sold in gallon jugs everywhere from auto parts stores to supermarkets. But be careful not to confuse the washer and coolant reservoirs. They should be marked with words or symbols. If not, check the remaining fluid in the reservoir—coolant is usually green, windshield washer solution is aqua. The coolant reservoir should have a hose leading to the top of the radiator. The washer reservoir's hose runs through the firewall to the windshield squirters.

## Upholstery Cleaning
Getting rid of the evidence

Unsightly stains on auto carpets and upholstery often don't respond to household cleaning methods because auto fabrics are treated with fire-retarding chemicals. The best cure is prevention. Treat all fabric upholstery and carpeting with a stain repellent when the car is new or at least clean. Dealers will do this for you (at great expense), or you can do it yourself with aerosol cans.

For the best results, remove all stains as soon as possible, before they set. Use only clean cloths or sponges, and switch to a clean area of the rag or sponge often as you clean. Open all windows when using cleaning fluids. If a ring forms after spot cleaning, clean the whole area immediately. Here's what to use on cloth upholstery:

| STAIN | REMOVAL TECHNIQUE |
| --- | --- |
| Blood, semen | Sponge off with cold water as soon as possible. Don't use soap; it may set the stain. |
| Food stains (black coffee, catsup, egg, juice, milk) | Carefully scrape off excess stain with a dull knife. Sponge stain with cold water. If necessary, rub lightly with cleaning fluid. |
| Greasy/oily stains (butter, coffee with cream, crayon, cosmetics, shoe polish, tar) | Carefully scrape off excess stain with a dull knife. Use cleaning fluid sparingly. |
| Ink | Blot as soon as possible with a rag dampened with rubbing alcohol. Repeat as necessary. Do not use ink eradicator, it will ruin the upholstery. |
| Sticky stains (candy, chili sauce, ice cream, mayonnaise) | Carefully scrape off excess stain with a dull knife. Sponge off with cool water and allow to dry. If some stain remains, use cleaning fluid sparingly. |
| Chewing gum | Harden gum with an ice cube, then scrape off as much as possible with a dull knife blade. Moisten residue with cleaning fluid and scrape some more. |

| | |
|---|---|
| Feces, urine, vomit | Quickly remove as much as possible with a paper towel. Sponge with cool water. Scrub lightly with warm water and mild soap. Rinse. If odor remains, treat area with a mixture of one teaspoon baking soda in one cup warm water. Rinse with clean, wet cloth. |
| Wine | Quickly remove as much as possible with sponge or paper towel. Dilute red wine immediately with club soda or tonic water and blot off. Cover spot with salt or baking soda; let dry and vacuum. |

## Cleaning other materials

| MATERIAL | CLEANING TECHNIQUE |
|---|---|
| Vinyl, leather | Use only warm water and mild soap. Let solution soak stain, then rub briskly with a clean, damp cloth. Repeat as needed. Use special leather cleaner on stubborn spots. |
| Suede | Only a qualified professional cleaning expert should attempt to clean suede. |
| Seat belts | Clean only with mild soap and warm water. Strong cleaners, bleach, or dye can weaken belts. |

# Upholstery Repairs
Keeping it all together

The repairs you can make on upholstery are quite limited. You can mend minor tears, but if seats are badly torn or worn out, cover them with seat covers or have the seats reupholstered professionally.

To fix a tear in vinyl upholstery, slip a patch of vinyl between the upholstery and the foam padding underneath. Apply auto trim or plastic adhesive to the patch and upholstery, then press the torn upholstery gently into place and let it dry. If you don't use a patch, the adhesive will eat into the foam seat padding.

Vinyl repair kits are available to patch small tears in vinyl seats, dashes, and tops. Never use adhesive tape; the adhesive will soften in the sun and then smear, staining both clothing and upholstery.

# V

## Vanity Plates
Getting your message across

Personalized license plates are now available, for an additional fee, in most states. You can get a plate that spells your name (if it has not already been taken), makes a statement about yourself or your car, or simply insults everyone who understands it. The examples given below come from actual license plates.

Names are quite popular. However, if that's what you want, you may have to settle for something like **RALPH 27**, because 26 other Ralphs got to the Department of Motor Vehicles before you.

You can also proclaim your profession, with plates like **CAVITY**, **SUBPOENA**, or **PP DOC**. Or you can sing the praises of your particular car; phrases like **BOBS ZCAR** are popular with owners of Nissan 300 ZX models, known to enthusiasts as Z-cars. Of course, you don't need a fancy car to sport a personalized plate; I've seen an old beater with the plate **ROCKBOTM**.

Which brings us to the space consideration. In many states you are limited to between six and eight numbers, letters, and/or spaces. But that need not stand in the way of creativity. Witness the Ferrari with the license **IXLR8** (I accelerate). You should try to avoid messages like **KISSYPOO**; there are enough perverts driving around without encouraging them. It's also wise not to flaunt such cop-baiting plates as **FLEWBYU**, **55 SUX**, and **HI OFFCR**.

You may even "monogram" your car by having your initials on the plate, such as **WAH** ("Wade A. Hoyt"). Some people include the whole family's initials—

**WHDHRHMH**—which is kind of tacky, but has the advantage of being difficult to read from a pursuing police car.

Motor vehicle bureaus try to screen out obscene and tasteless messages, even in a foreign language, although **MERDE** got through in one state.

If you want a personalized plate, write to your state Department of Motor Vehicles. Ask about the fee and the number of letters available; find out if the higher fee must be paid annually or just once. Be prepared to list a second and third choice. Somebody's already got **B4 TAX**, **RU RICH 2**, **GAS PIG**, **AUDI DO D**, **SO SU ME**, **NO WIFE**, **GR8 2SH**, and **6UL DV8**.

# Warning Lights

Idiot's delight?

When warning lights first began to appear on dashboards in place of instruments, they were called "idiot lights" by car buffs who thought they were only for people too stupid to read conventional gauges. In fact, warning lights serve a very useful purpose by immediately calling the driver's attention to an abnormal condition. Many sports cars with a full complement of instruments also have warning lights for their attention-getting qualities.

The first warning lights were fairly straightforward and easy to decipher. TEMP meant that the coolant temperature was too high and the engine was in danger of overheating. OIL meant that the oil pressure was too low, and the engine should be shut off immediately to avoid damage. ALT or BAT meant that the alternator was not keeping up with electrical demand and that the battery was being drained.

Today's warning lights are more complex, but they are all explained in your Owner's Manual. Most warning lights come on briefly when the engine is being started (to show that their bulbs are working), and then shut off—unless there is trouble. Here's what some of the new messages mean:

ENGINE combines the functions of the old OIL and TEMP lights. This is unfortunate because, if the engine is overheating, you should rev it slightly to circulate more coolant through the block; but if the oil pressure is too low, you should turn the engine off at once to avoid damaging it. Separate lights allow you to make this important distinction; with an ENGINE light, you have no choice but to shut off the engine.

ABS or ANTI-LOCK means that the anti-lock brake system is malfunctioning, and the brakes have reverted to conventional operation. This is not a disabling emergency, but you should have the brake system checked soon to restore ABS operation (see BRAKES, ANTI-LOCK).

BRAKE means that the parking brake is on, or that one of the two brake circuits is not operating, usually because brake fluid is leaking (see BRAKE FAILURE).

CHECK ENGINE or SERVICE ENGINE SOON means that the engine's operating computer has detected a fault and has stored a "trouble code" in its memory. A mechanic with the proper equipment can trigger a readout of the trouble code and quickly find the problem. If the SERVICE ENGINE light comes on, yet the car seems to be running fine, you needn't call for a tow truck. Just make an appointment to have a dealer or well-equipped shop check the car.

Some cars have lights that come on, or little flags that pop up to cover the odometer with such obscure messages as SENSOR, O2 SENS, EGR, or EMISSIONS. These signals come on at specific service intervals to indicate that parts of the pollution control system, such as the exhaust oxygen sensor or the EGR valve, need to be inspected, serviced, or repaired. Not all cars have these little wonders, so check your Owner's Manual.

TURBO means that the turbocharger is malfunctioning and may damage the engine (see TURBOCHARGER). Shut off the engine immediately.

In addition to these lights, some cars have warnings for such things as low oil, windshield washer, or coolant levels, burned out exterior lights, low fuel, or if a door, trunk, or hatch is ajar. One Maserati model has 29 warning lights. The only light missing in some cars is one that tells when the next payment is due!

## Warranties
### Getting them honored

The first thing to remember here is that car companies issue warranties to protect themselves, not consumers. A warranty limits the manufacturer's liability to specific items for specific periods of time. After that, it's your tough luck. Because most buyers don't see it that way, long warranties have become a marketing tool. However, there is less to a five-, six-, or seven-year warranty than first meets the eye.

Many car dealers hate to do warranty work because they feel the factory doesn't compensate them fairly. Quick, simple jobs are not a problem; but if you have a job that requires complex trouble-shooting or major parts replacement, you may get the runaround from some dealers.

When a dealer replaces parts under warranty, they are returned to the factory for inspection. If they prove to be OK, the dealer will not be reimbursed for the parts or labor. It's no wonder some dealers give cars with warranty complaints the "sunshine treatment": you bring your car to the dealership in the morning, they park it outside all day, then return it in the evening, having done nothing but proclaiming it fixed.

The first step toward getting a warranty honored is to understand it. The typical car is covered by several different warranties:

The *Basic Warranty* covers most parts of the car and the labor required to repair them, usually for 12 to 36 months or 12,000 to 36,000 miles, whichever comes first. Parts scheduled for periodic replacement (like filters) or subject to normal wear (such as windshield wiper blades, brake linings, etc.) are not usually covered.

Tires, radio, and the battery may be covered by separate warranties from their manufacturers. You can find these warranties in the glove compartment of a new car.

The *Powertrain Warranty* is usually longer than the Basic Warranty—up to seven years or 100,000 miles on some cars—but covers fewer parts. This warranty varies from car to car, but usually covers most parts of the engine, transmission, and differential, plus the drive shafts and U-joints. Some parts of the powertrain, like the carburetor or fuel-injection system, are not covered, so be sure to read the fine print carefully.

The *Corrosion Warranty* usually guarantees to replace *or repair* (at the manufacturer's option) body parts actually perforated by rust. That is, there has to be a hole completely through the bodywork. So-called *cosmetic* rust or blistered paint is not covered, even if it makes your car look awful. The repair option is a cop-out because many patch jobs rust through again in a year or less, and you don't get a second repair under most warranties.

The *Emissions Performance Warranty* is required by federal law. It guarantees that your car (if properly maintained) will pass any state emissions inspection that meets EPA requirements for two years or 24,000 miles. This warranty includes the carburetor, fuel-injection system, and ignition parts, as well as the parts listed below.

The *Emissions Defect Warranty* (also government-required) covers all emission control equipment on your car for five years or 50,000 miles. The replacement or repair must be borne by the car maker if (1) an emission control part fails due to a defect in materials or workmanship or (2) a malfunction causes your car to exceed federal (not state) emissions standards.

Part (2) is the "catch 22" here. If your carburetor or fuel-injection system malfunctions, your car may well fail a state emission control inspection. But car makers consider carburetors "a gray area" since they are not, in fact, emission control equipment. Putting an individual car through a federal emissions test to prove that it doesn't meet the standards can cost many times more than the repair. On the other hand, if a catalytic converter, EGR valve, or other pollution control gizmo fails, it is clearly covered.

*Extended Warranties* (sometimes called service contracts) are actually insurance policies sold by car makers and "aftermarket" insurers to fill some of the gaps in the standard warranties listed above. But be wary—their coverage varies widely, and some of them may prove useless when you need them, years after their purchase, if the issuing company has gone out of business. If you buy an extended warranty, deal only with well-established firms.

Every warranty has conditions you must meet to keep the warranty in effect. For example, you must change oil and filters at specified intervals, perform other routine maintenance, and for most cars, use only unleaded gas. To keep the warranty valid, you *must* perform the maintenance specified in your Owner's Manual and keep dated receipts or other records to prove it. You may have the work done by your dealer or an independent garage, or do it yourself, as long as you have those dated receipts. (If you buy oil and filters yourself, it is assumed you used them unless there is evidence to the contrary.)

Many powertrain and extended warranties have a deductible that requires you to pay the first $100 or so of the repair cost.

Warranties are sometimes transferable to a second owner for a hefty registration fee—often $100.

Once you have digested and understood all the fine print, you are ready to get that warranty honored. If all doesn't go well after the first trip to the dealer, see the advice listed under COMPLAINTS, CONSUMER GROUPS, LEMON LAWS, MECHANICS, REPAIRS, and TECHNICAL SERVICE BULLETINS. Don't be belligerent—give the dealer a chance to do the job right. If your dealer knows early in the game that you understand the rules, you will be more likely to get better-than-average service.

# Warranties, Secret
Serving some of the people some of the time

Car makers sometimes repair cars for free or at a reduced cost after the official warranty has expired. This is done either as a goodwill gesture or to avoid the possibility of legal action. However, these extra-warranty repairs may not be voluntarily offered to every customer suffering the problem, perhaps because the dealer is not aware of the extension, or because the manufacturer wants to oil only the "squeaky wheels."

Car companies never use the words "secret warranty." They prefer euphemisms like "policy adjustment" or "goodwill gesture." Most policy adjustments are spelled out in technical service bulletins (TSBs) that are sent to dealers but are often misfiled or unread. If a dealer tells you that a certain repair is not covered by your warranty, ask him to check his TSB file for a policy adjustment. If that doesn't give you satisfaction, ask to speak to the Zone Manager and contact the NHTSA (see TECHNICAL SERVICE BULLETINS).

Policy adjustments are sometimes made only for those who complain the loudest and longest (see COMPLAINTS).

## Washing and Waxing
### More than keeping up appearances

Neglected cars not only look old before their time, but get old faster than cars that are properly cared for. Car care is not only mechanical, but cosmetic as well. Regular washing and waxing keeps the paint in good shape and helps to prevent rust.

It doesn't much matter whether you wash your car by hand or take it to a car wash. Old-style bristle brushes in some car washes can be abrasive to paint, but new "brushless" emporiums (the brushes are made of cloth strips rather than bristles) may be better than hand washing. Unless you use as much rinse water as the car wash, you may be abrading the paint with dust and grit when you wash by hand. New "touchless" car washes use high-pressure jets of water that sometimes pry off loose trim or penetrate marginal weatherstripping. In areas where roads are salted to remove winter ice and snow, use a car wash that rinses the underside of the car with water that has *not* been recycled.

If you wash your car by hand, do it in the shade and use plenty of rinse water before, after, and while you wash the car. Start by hosing out the wheel wells and the underside of the car. Use a soft brush, mild soap, and a garden hose (or the pressure wand at a self-service car wash). Remove all salt and impacted road dirt from the wheel wells, under the bumpers and doors, and inside each door opening. Do a small area at a time, rinse off all soap, and check for rust spots (see PAINT TOUCH-UP). Use an old soft toothbrush to clean the grille and other crevices. Dry the car with a clean chamois that has been soaked in clear water and wrung out.

The shelves of auto parts stores are piled high with a confusing array of polishes, waxes, cleaners, and compounds with conflicting claims. Here is what you need:

*Bug and tar remover* (usually a kerosene mixture) does what it says without harming paint. Use it for stubborn spots you encounter while you wash, then rinse it off completely. When removing tree sap, let it soak for awhile to soften it.

*Wheel cleaners* are specially formulated to remove stubborn, black, disc brake dust from aluminum or mag wheels.

*Cleaner or polish* is a very mild abrasive that removes the "dead" oxidized paint layer called chalk. Chalking is caused by exposure to the elements. You can buy cleaner or polish separately and do twice the work, or buy a combination cleaner/wax and do both jobs at once.

*Polishing compound* is a stronger abrasive used to restore badly chalked and faded paint that's been neglected. This is a paste (usually white, to distinguish it from the still stronger rubbing compound) which should be applied by hand. Use a damp cloth and light pressure to avoid removing too much paint, especially on sharp edges of the bodywork.

*Rubbing compound* is a harsh abrasive, usually red or pink, used as a last resort to having a new paint job. It should be used with great caution, lest you rub away all of the color coat and penetrate into the primer, in which case you will need to repaint. Metallic and clear-coat paintjobs are easily ruined with inexpert use of either compound.

*Wax* comes in hard solid form, soft paste, liquid, and sprays. The harder the wax, the more difficult it is to apply. In general, they all last about as long, except for some sprays, which are diluted to allow spraying. Wax fills in the microscopic crevices in weathered paint, and keeps water, air, and pollution away from the paint so that it doesn't chalk. Rain will form almost spherical droplets on a newly-waxed car. As the wax wears off, the water beads become larger and flatter, a signal that it's time to re-wax.

*Polymer sealant* is the stuff that new car dealers call "sealer-protectant" and charge $100 or more to apply. You can buy it for $20 or less in auto parts stores and apply it like wax, which is about what it is—an extra long-lasting wax. Some labels claim that after using a polymer sealant you shouldn't have to wax the car for years.

*Silicone protectant* gives a satisfying shine to leather, rubber, and plastics, including vinyl. You just spray the stuff on, spread it around, let it soak in, and sop up any excess. It repels water, oxygen, ozone, and ultra violet rays, and forms an anti-static film that helps repel dust. It gives tire sidewalls that deep-black showroom look, but don't use it on tire treads or you'll have a skidmobile! Likewise, leather seats will become slippery—one more reason to buckle up.

No wash-and-wax job is complete without thoroughly vacuuming the interior. Remove floormats for cleaning. Clean carpets and fabric seats with a foaming shampoo (see UPHOLSTERY STAINS). Use a cotton-tipped swab dipped in household cleaner to get into those little vents and crevices on the dash. Use a glass cleaner such as Windex on all windows, especially inside, where film collects from smoke, and from vapors that escape from vinyl and other plastics.

# Wheel Alignment
Let's get something straight

If your car pulls to one side on level roads, the steering wheel shimmies, or the tires wear unevenly, the wheels may need to be aligned. On many cars, the wheel angles can be adjusted in three directions, namely caster, camber, and toe-in. Toe-in can be adjusted on all cars. On some cars with MacPherson strut suspensions, caster and camber cannot be adjusted. On many front-drive cars, the angles of the rear wheels can also be adjusted on a special four-wheel alignment machine.

Wheel alignment should be checked at least once a year or if your car develops any of the symptoms listed above. Hitting a curb, pothole, or bad bump can throw the wheels out of alignment.

Car makers issue wheel alignment specifications for all cars. Have any work done at a shop that specializes in alignment and has modern four-wheel alignment racks with precision measuring devices.

Some shops will attempt to adjust camber and caster on MacPherson strut suspensions by bending the struts. This is not recommended by any car maker. Again, choose your mechanic with care.

## Wheel Balancing
### Getting rid of the shakes

Irregularities in wheels and tires cause them to shimmy at certain speeds, leading to uneven tire wear. Professional wheel balancing—crimping small lead weights to the wheel rim—compensates for these irregularities. The wheels should be balanced whenever a tire is removed from a wheel and remounted, when new tires are installed, or if you notice steering wheel shimmy or uneven tire wear.

Tires and wheels should be *dynamically* balanced on machines that spin the tire and wheel at high speeds. Self-adhesive balance weights should be used on aluminum, alloy, or mag wheels, which can be damaged by crimping weights to their rims. Be sure to have all five wheels balanced, including the spare.

If more than four ounces of weight is needed to balance a wheel and tire, the wheel may be bent or the tire defective. If a wheel still shimmies after it has been balanced, find a shop that's equipped to spin-balance the wheel on the car. This procedure can spot bad wheel bearings, hubs, and out-of-balance brake rotors or drums.

# Windshield Washers
## Keeping them squirting

Keep the windshield washer reservoir filled with a pre-mixed cleaning solution containing a mild detergent that will not streak paint, plus antifreeze to keep the system working in the winter. If the washer system is not working, the wipers alone will smear road film or light rain, dangerously cutting your vision.

The typical system consists of a plastic reservoir and electric pump in the engine compartment, connected by flexible plastic tubing to spray nozzles on the hood, cowl, or windshield wiper arms. When the washer doesn't work, it's usually out of fluid, but the nozzles may also be clogged or the tubing crimped, split, or disconnected.

Use a needle to clear dirt from clogged nozzles. Some reservoirs have filter screens at the bottom of the pickup tube that runs to the pump. You can clear a clogged screen by flushing it with warm water and/or blowing through it in the direction opposite from the usual fluid flow.

You can correct the aim of a misdirected ball-type nozzle by inserting a needle into the spray orifice and using it as a handle to swivel the nozzle. Tubular nozzles can be carefully bent with pliers to aim them. Fluid-control nozzles (which look like tiny plastic boxes) and wiper-mounted nozzles cannot be re-aimed.

If the pump motor won't run, check the fuse box (see FUSES) or see a mechanic.

If the pump runs and the nozzles seem clear, but fluid will not come out, remove the tubing from the nozzle and operate the washer switch. If fluid comes out of the tube, the nozzle is still clogged. If fluid does not come out, check the tubing for kinks, cracks, or disconnected junctions. Replace any defective tubing. If only the ends are cracked, you may have enough extra length to cut off the cracked part and reinstall the tubing. If the tubing is clogged, disconnect both ends of each tube and flush it with warm water, using a syringe.

If the system still won't squirt, disconnect the tubing at the pump and operate the switch. If no fluid comes out, the pickup tube is still blocked or disconnected (check again) or the pump is defective. Buy a new one or have a replacement installed.

## Windshield Wipers
Keeping your vision clear

Wipers work best when you keep both the glass and the rubber wiper squeegee clean. Wash them with a window washing solution like Windex or with washer fluid. Wipe the squeegees clean with a paper towel to remove all grit that causes streaks. If streaking continues, replace the rubber squeegees or the entire wiper blade assemblies.

Replacement squeegees, called refills, are the least expensive but a bit tricky to install. You must remove a retaining clip or press a release button, then pull out the old squeegee, thread in its replacement, and replace the clip.

Squeegees are sold in several lengths, from a nominal 13 inches to 16 inches. You must buy the length and type of squeegee required for your car. It's a good idea to bring the old squeegee to the auto parts store so you can compare it to the replacements offered. Rear wipers are often a different size from the windshield wipers; bring both.

The metal and rubber wiper blade assembly clips or snaps onto the wiper arm via a single connector. Unfortunately, there are five popular connector designs, so you must buy not only the right length blade, but one with the right connector as well. The box the blade comes in should have complete instructions for removing and installing the blade, a finicky process that may involve release buttons or levers, spring catches, locking posts, retaining springs, and other devices designed more to avoid other patents than for user convenience.

Squeegees are made of natural rubber, which deteriorates from exposure and abrasion. In most populous (polluted) areas, squeegees need to be replaced every 6 to 12 months. In the winter, snow and ice can clog the joints of the metal blade assembly, preventing it from flexing to follow the contours of the glass. You can buy special winter blades to prevent this—the entire blade assembly is encased in rubber to keep out ice, snow, and moisture.

## Winter Driving
How to get on the road and stay there

The first step for successful winter driving is to winterize your car (see below). Next, make sure you can see and be seen. Check that all lights are working and their lenses are clean. Inspect wipers and washers, and make sure the washer reservoir is filled with fluid that contains washer antifreeze. Carry a jug of extra washer fluid in the trunk; it gets used up at an incredible rate in bad weather.

Check the operation of defrosters and defoggers

before you need them. Carry galoshes, extra gloves, an ice scraper and brush for the windows, aerosol de-icer, tire chains (if you use them), jumper cables, a bag of sand, and a small shovel in the trunk for emergencies. If you can avoid it, don't drive when it's snowing heavily; stay home until the roads have been cleared.

Before you drive, start the engine, put the defroster and defogger on HIGH, and clear *all* windows and lights of ice and snow (see DE-ICING WINDOWS). Adjust your seat and clothing so that you are comfortable behind the wheel and can reach all controls.

Stopping distances and traction decrease on snow and ice, making driving more difficult. Leave extra distance for stopping and passing under these conditions. Drive smoothly when roads are slick, being careful to avoid sudden acceleration, sharp turns, or hard braking, all of which can cause a skid.

To climb a steep hill, you must gain e ugh momentum to get to the top before you reach the hill, then cruise uphill without depressing the gas pedal further. If you have to floor the gas pedal part way up the hill, the wheels will spin and you may lose control (see SKID CONTROL).

If your wiper blades clog with ice, the wipers will streak and you won't be able to see. Pull off the road in a safe, clear spot (if you can find one) and bang the blades up and down against the windshield several times to dislodge ice. If you can't find a plowed spot, don't stop; pulling off the road in an unfamiliar area may drop you into an unseen snow-filled ditch. Drive slowly and open the window. Lean forward and place your hand on the outside of the windshield so the wiper can run up onto your fingers. It will be cold, but it won't hurt. Flip the wiper away from the glass; when it snaps back down, the ice will crack and fall off. Don't attempt this if you can't steer a steady course at the same time, or while driving at high speeds.

## Winterizing
Getting ready for the big one

Many areas of the car require special maintenance before cold weather sets in to assure reliable operation.

*Cooling system* should be drained and flushed each Fall and filled with the proper percentage of antifreeze (see ANTIFREEZE). Check drive belts and radiator hoses and replace any that are in bad shape (see BELTS and HOSES).

*Electrical system* has to be in top shape for winter, when engines are hardest to start because the oil gets thicker and the battery weaker in cold weather. Check the battery cables and state of charge (see BATTERY CHECKS), and have the engine tuned up in the Fall rather than the traditional Spring tuneup.

*Exhaust system* should be in perfect shape for the cold weather to come, when you will be driving with the windows closed. The smallest leak in the muffler or exhaust pipes can lead to carbon monoxide poisoning.

*Tires* are even more vital in winter than they are the rest of the year. Check their pressure and condition more often in winter (see TIRE PRESSURE and TIRE REPLACEMENT). If you change to winter tires each Fall (see SNOW TIRES), that's a good time to rotate tires (see TIRE ROTATION).

Safe winter driving starts with a safe car.

# Z

# Zippers
Keep them sliding right along

The renaissance of convertibles has also brought a return of automotive zippers, usually used around the plastic rear window of a fabric top. On a few cars, the upholstery is fitted over the seat padding with zippers.

When zippers refuse to zip, the usual causes are corrosion (on metal zippers) or a slider that comes off the tracks. Lubricate the teeth of a metal zipper periodically with small amounts of a silicone lubricant, being careful to keep it off the fabric.

Sliders will come off the track if the stops at either end are missing, or if one or more teeth are broken. To fix this, you must first get the slider back on track. Use needle-nose pliers to pry open and remove the staple that serves as a stop at the bottom of a metal zipper. Pull the slider all the way down and carefully thread the loose track of teeth through the open hole of the slider. Make sure the two rows of teeth are aligned at the bottom, then push the slider well up the zipper.

Replace the staple and crimp it shut with the pliers. If the staple is damaged or lost, you can make a new stop by stitching the bottom few teeth together with extra-heavy thread. You can do the same with a missing top stop.

To remove the molded-in stop from a flat plastic zipper, you have to cut it off. Use a soldering iron to make a new stop, either by melting a new piece of plastic onto the teeth, or by fusing a few teeth together.

Plastic coil zippers are seldom used on cars because they are relatively weak. But if you do have one and it pulls apart, you can get its act together simply by pulling the slider down and back up again.

# Author! Author!

Wade and Roy are a couple of good ol' boys whom publisher Paul Wahl has known since his free-lance journalist days in the Sixties. The authors got together for lunch at New York's Cafe des Artistes and, amid the inspiring Howard Chandler Christy murals, decided to collaborate on *Driver's Survival Handbook*. Their unique talents and expertise really show in these pages.

**Wade Hoyt**, now Editor of Hearst's prestigious automotive journal, *Motor,* always wanted to be a writer on cars and driving. He prepared for that career by studying journalism and mechanical engineering at Queens College, City University of New York, graduating with the Class of 1965.

During the following twenty-odd years, he has been Assistant Home & Shop Editor of *Mechanix Illustrated*, Managing Editor of *Science & Mechanics,* Automotive Editor of *Popular Mechanics,* and Project Director for the Reader's Digest General Books Division, where he created the best-selling *Complete Car Care Manual.* As a free lance, Hoyt has contributed many automotive articles to major national magazines such as *Cosmopolitan, Esquire, Family Circle, New York, Penthouse, Popular Science, Road & Track,* and *TV Guide.*

Presently, he is serving his second term as President of the International Motor Press Association and also is a member of the Society of Automotive Engineers.

In his work, Hoyt travels around the world, visiting automobile factories and test driving their latest products. So vast is his experience that he can say "I've driven just about everything but a Skoda."

**Roy Doty** is a world-famous illustrator who began his career as a U.S. Army cartoonist in the 1940's. Three times, his peers in the National Cartoonists Society have voted him "Illustrator of the Year" and he has won numerous Art Director awards too.

For more than 35 years, Doty's "Wordless Workshop" has been the most-read monthly feature in *Popular Science* and his latest cartoon, "Eureka!", now appears regularly in *Family Circle.* He is a frequent contributor to a wide range of other magazines including *Field & Stream, Golf Digest,* and *Tennis.* Doty has written and illustrated over 100 books with sales totalling in the millions.

A lifelong car buff, his collection has included an early MG-TC, a 1929 Bugatti, a 1948 Lincoln Continental convertible, five Porsches, and three Alfa Romeos.